Russ...

Endorsement

"From Noah to the apostle Paul, Russell Young reveals the pathway to godly wisdom and the blessings of living it in the trenches of everyday life."

—Pastor Jon Kraner

The author challenges our pursuit of knowledge with a good read on wisdom for all willing to dig further into one of the most significant subjects of our divine-human relationship.

If God is God, then we need to be revering Him for a more amicable association: Living in the Wisdom of

God's Holy Word.

—Gus Christo-Baker

Living *in the* Wisdom *of* GOD'S Holy Word

Russell Young

Living *in the* Wisdom *of* GOD'S Holy Word

TATE PUBLISHING
AND ENTERPRISES, LLC

Published by Tate Publishing & Enterprises, LLC
127 E. Trade Center Terrace | Mustang, Oklahoma 73064 USA
1.888.361.9473 | www.tatepublishing.com

Tate Publishing is committed to excellence in the publishing industry. The company reflects the philosophy established by the founders, based on Psalm 68:11,
"The Lord gave the word and great was the company of those who published it."

Book design copyright © 2015 by Tate Publishing, LLC. All rights reserved.
Cover design by Jeffrey Doblados
Interior design by Caypeeline Casas

Published in the United States of America

ISBN: 978-1-68142-945-8
Religion / Christian Life / Spiritual Growth
15.07.29

Acknowledgments

༄ঌ৵ঌ

Supposing it would suddenly become possible to use a single word to describe my feelings about the writing of this book. That magnificent word would be GRATITUDE.

I am indeed deeply grateful for the encouragement, the loving support, the intelligence, and the ability of so many people. Actually, they are too numerous to mention, but most especially I will cite my grandson, Joshua Eliakim Miller II, his wife Christina, and her brother Le Wayne Ebert (a Pre-med student at Western Carolina University). I am deeply grateful to my wife JoAnn for her enduring patience, technical assistance, and for her abiding love.

Having survived through seventy years of the 20th century, and now fifteen years of the 21st century, I have witnessed the ravages that have been wreaked upon this planet as a result of our lack of genuine, God given WISDOM!

Yes, our very lives, our survival is in danger. It has reached the point where our human minds must grasp the fact that without God's Holy WISDOM, without the power given to us by the Holy Spirit, we are indeed doomed to destruction.

This book speaks to the yearning of our souls to seek His wisdom – our only hope for survival. We believers, all truly born-again Christians, must strive diligently to discover the wonder and delight of God's WISDOM as found in the inspired words of these pages.

With the ageless WISDOM found here, we must join others in sharing it, taking it deeper into their hearts and souls, and applying it to everything that we say and do in our everyday existence.

I am dedicating this book to increasing the Power, through His Spiritually endowed WISDOM, in each of our lives. Let each of us, with the nourishment of this WISDOM, become nourishment for those around us, in our communities, our country, and for our entire world. As we receive His WISDOM, let us let our light shine throughout the universe. AMEN

Contents

∽⊗∾

Prologue

Wisdom in the Word: Spoken by prophets, alive in Christ

Throughout this book, I shall try to clarify for you once and for all the true meaning of the word *wisdom*. Just as in the word *kingdom*, we have "king" dom—the reign of the Almighty God, and in the word "wis" dom—the Word of the Almighty God.

Wisdom comes to us by way of the Word of God as spoken by the patriarchs, prophets, kings, and apostles of the New Testament. Simply put, it is my goal to lead the young and the not-so-young to begin to gain God's wisdom through His Word, to develop moral insight and strength, to live out their lives in eternal bliss, accepting the everlasting joy of His inner peace by means of a life centered and focused upon a life drawn ever closer to a loving and abiding relationship with the Savior Jesus Christ.

My friend, King Solomon himself, obviously realized something that we often forget: knowledge can be gained through study, power can be acquired by conquest, and honor can be obtained by deeds of greatness. Wisdom, however, is a gift from God! James 1:5 tells us that anyone who lacks wisdom should ask God, who "gives generously to all without finding fault."

Could it just be that the key to man's wisdom is the fact that he must realize he needs it?

It seems to me that we too often depend upon ourselves—our instincts, our training, our education, even our reputation—rather than looking to God for wisdom.

Look at it this way: being wise does not mean knowing everything, memorizing large portions of Scripture, or having a list of degrees by your name; it means being able to see situations from God's point of view and being able to recognize our limitations.

What do we get when we seek wisdom? Well, most often we get more questions—lots of very hard questions, many more questions than answers—but those questions drive us back to God. Dependence upon the Almighty God is the ultimate wisdom!

We find Proverbs 23:23, "Buy the truth, and do not sell it; get wisdom, discipline, and understanding." Need an example? A friend of mine was in need of a new cell phone. He found the one he wanted, and the price was right—$180. He jumped at the chance. It worked just fine for a couple of weeks. Then, he began to have difficulty with the reception. After that, he couldn't receive calls at all. Final[1] he lost the ability to use any parts of the phone. He realized then that he had been duped. They had made a fool of him.

Dear friend, there are many things in our lives that look good but are actually really inferior. Fame, wealth, prestige, looks all seem to be wonderful things to have, but they soon fade away and leave us with nothing.

Truth, wisdom, and understanding are costly, but they are worth anything that we have to give. They fill us with inner treasures which will never fade. There is nothing greater in this world to which we can devote ourselves.

Dear reader, God will guide us to wisdom; all we need to do is ask Him. He blesses anyone who sincerely tries to find truth. With God on our side, we can rest assured that we can attain our goal. Once that goal is attained, we will never let go of the riches of wisdom and understanding with which we have been blessed.

Throughout this book, you will learn from patriarchs, kings, prophets, and apostles just how God's wisdom makes our lives complete and keeps us on the path to eternal bliss with Him. To illustrate this point, I would like to tell of some experience that my brother had in his career as a chief petty officer in the United States Navy. He explained to me that the art of navigation depends largely upon the existence of fixed points. He said that the fixed point can be a lighthouse, or even a star up in the heavens. It doesn't really matter what it is, but it must be fixed and solid. The navigator takes his bearings and steers his course by the truth of the fixed point. He cannot take his bearing from a cloud—it moves, or even disappears. Navigation is possible because of the existence of a fixed course.

Now, dear friend, you can see that the voyage of life is like that—you must have fixed points from which to take a bearing. The attributes of God are fixed points. Wisdom is given to us to keep our lives on the heavenly course. What are those attributes? They are His love, His faithfulness, His justice, His purity, His holiness, His power, to name a few. They are all the fixed points, the established parts of God's eternal nature.

The more we focus on these points and the more we understand them, the more safely and securely we will make our way across the "sea of life." You will definitely find that many things in life will change, but never the attributes and nature of Almighty God. What He was, He is, and what He is, He was, and what He was and is, He ever will be—world without end!

Now, I'll suggest that we must keep reminding ourselves of the things which are absolutely certain, entirely beyond doubt. We must keep reassuring ourselves that God is not like the gods whom the nonbelievers worship or idols they have made for themselves, but that He is everlasting, without beginning, and without end.

God is the self-existing one, the eternal "I AM." This means He is dependent upon no one or anything for His existence. God is absolutely righteous—another fixed point. When we focus upon that fixed point, our view of God becomes much bigger, and problems become smaller and much less meaningful.

Yes, we must keep in mind that God is self-existent. He is holy, He is absolutely righteous, and He is faithful. Remember: God is the God of the covenant. He renewed it with David. God was bound and committed to His chosen people (which include you and me) in a covenant relationship that can never be broken. God cannot and will not do anything that is contrary to His character. So, I ask you: why get all bent out of shape? Focus on the fixed points. Gaze upon His glorious attributes.

If, on the voyage of life, we need fixed points from which to take our bearings, then we Christians have the most reliable of them all, and among them are the goodness and the graciousness of God.

Wisdom for the Voyage of Life

"Here in the darkness of this world today,
Tossed and buffeted by the sinful flood,
Attached to His spiritual soul—I pray,
'I love you, Lord, for you are good!'"

—Russell Young

Dear reader, the most glorious light, the one we seek above all, is spiritual light, and for this light, the Bible is our only reliable guide. The Bible contains the mind of God; it shows us the condition of man and the way to His salvation. It exposes the disillusionment of sinners plus the joy of true believers. The better we know and understand the Word of God, the more likely we are to find the spiritual light that God shines on our souls. Every word of Scripture is true, and its teachings are unchangeable.

No matter how dark the world grows around us, the Bible shows us that paradise is restored, Heaven is opened to us, and the gates of hell are revealed. Christ is its significant one, and the glory of God is emphasized throughout.

Read the Word to be wise and practice it that your life may be holy. In the Bible, you will find a gold mine of inspiration and an ocean of pleasure. Study it and fill your memory with His Word. Le its Word control every beat of your heart and guide you in every step of your life. The wise person will read the Bible slowly, frequently, and, by all means, prayerfully. Many lives have been transformed through the study of His living, loving Word. It will happen to you as you draw ever nearer to Him.

My friend, our problems often seem to be overwhelming because we allow things to seem larger in our own eyes than in eternal truths. A little dime, when held close to your eye, can blot out the sun. Through His Holy Word, we will learn not to glance at things but to gaze at God. Seeing God clearly will enable us to see all other things clearly.

Yes, truer words could never be spoken. The Holy Bible contains the absolute epitome of wisdom. Proverbs 1:7 says, "The fear of the Lord is the beginning of knowledge, but fools despise wisdom and discipline."

My friend, I am well aware of the fact that most of you, dear readers, are parents. I personally have two children, four grandchildren, and twelve great-grandchildren. I feel that I must assume some of the responsibility of creating love and obedience in their lives. I realize that I can only accomplish this by obeying God's Holy Word and by staking my life on His truths. I fully realize that before I can give them advice on "what is right and just and fair," I must emphasize the value of the wisdom that leads to a life that is in obedience to God's Holy Word. The goal of my advice is to give them some spiritual insight concerning wisdom, knowledge, and understanding.

By wisdom, I am not referring to academic achievement. The true test of knowledge goes beyond academics to moral responsibility. Decision-making shows up in the disciplining of the character, which leads to a prudent and disciplined life. Living a prudent life means the decisions made are controlled by an understanding between right and wrong. Therefore, I help them to make wise choices—that is, to tell the truth rather than lies; to respect the property of others rather than take for themselves; to keep from hurting others; to hold the miracle of life in the highest regard.

Remember: the home is the greenhouse where godly wisdom is cultivated. The power of Christian living in a family relationship is the classroom for true Christianity. When a home is blessed with true Christian spirituality, each person develops a servant's attitude. We must recognize the fact that one filled with the spirit of Christ will strongly desire to serve. He does not grab on to his own emotional territory, but lifts and encourages other family members through his Christian spirit.

By reading this book, *Living in the Wisdom of the Word of God*, I pray that you will be a good role model and teach the importance of knowing and obeying Jesus Christ, knowing and displaying godly character, loving each other in the family, and working hard to contribute effectively to their living and loving character. In 2 Chronicles 16:9, it says, "For the eyes of the Lord range through the earth to strengthen those whose hearts are fully committed to Him!"

It is true that the faithful among us are indeed well aware of the fact that wisdom comes from unexpected places in unexpected ways. Wisdom does not come with a loud noise, but with a whisper. I am writing this book to help people increase their faith in God and to show the way for them to be instructed, encouraged, even stimulated to develop a deeper faith in Christ. This deeper faith will give all Christians a stronger foundation, fixed point, and bolster their thinking concerning a life of security today and on to eternity with the Lord. Faith is life combined with wisdom; it shows how one feels, thinks, talks, and acts. Jesus said, "I do nothing myself. I do only what pleases the Father!" This is true humanness; the Christian, through the Holy Spirit within, will allow Christ to work in him through wisdom and faith.

People throughout the world, even here in the great United States of America, have been living in unbelief and disobedience. My prayer is that they will soon be changing their ways toward a better future. This is God's Grace at work in the world, His gracious direction; when God moves, we must follow. For hundreds of years, even thousands, God's creative plans have been in place from Adam and Eve to Abraham, Moses, Joshua, to our own Savior

Jesus Christ, God's Word—His wisdom—has been our joyous blessing.

Finally, it is my sincere prayer that God may speak to you through his book. Wisdom does come to us from unexpected places in unexpected ways. Pray to God that He might bestow His blessings upon you and that He will faithfully answer your call. My prayer is that through this little book on wisdom, you will find the love of God with more passion and with more depth than ever before.

Amen and Amen.

THE PATRIARCHS IN THE BIBLE

Noah

In Genesis, we read: "The Lord saw how great man's wickedness on the earth had become, and that every inclination of the thoughts of his heart was only evil all of the time." Yes, to the Lord, it appeared that every thought coming from man was absolutely evil "all of the time." These words give the reason for the flood, which was the first activity of the punishing judgment of God. God never acts in such judgment until it is necessary to fulfill his highest purposes of humanity. And whenever it is necessary, God does act.

And yet, we find that "Noah found a favor in the eyes of the Lord." Why? How could this be? It was because Noah was a righteous man. In spite of all the other people, Noah was without blame. Noah walked with God. He was not violent and corrupt, as were the rest of the people on earth. It was at this point that God had seen enough. He commanded Noah to build an ark of safety for him and his entire family.

If you are not careful, you can almost forget that Bible heroes were real men living in a real age. But Noah was a real man, and he did live in a real age—building a boat longer than a football field in a land that had never seen rain, preaching God's grace against impending doom for 120 years without a single convert outside his own family, and feeling his neighbors slanderous attitudes against him for his insinuation that they were the ones in need of help.

True, Noah lived in those days of darkness, sin, violence, and corruption. Noah was given an opportunity to escape from the darkness. That opportunity came from the power of Light—the wisdom—that comes from our faith in the Almighty God, and through the power of the Holy Spirit, the darkness is overcome.

This then is the result of living the life of righteousness—walking in God's wisdom and remaining always at God's side. Thus, our darkness becomes light, and our world finds favor in the eyes of the Lord once again. Jesus said, "I am the light of the world," and we also are, for He said in His very own words: "You are the light of the world. A city on a hill cannot be hidden."

Dear friend, our light must come from Him if we are to overcome the darkness in the world. Therefore, let us treat the present worldly darkness as an opportunity and devote our lives to be wholly like Christ. We must forsake everything that keeps us from being faithful, living daily in His righteousness as we walk with Him.

The Holy Spirit will guide us and direct us, and with His wisdom, we shall find His light to lead us out of this violent and sinful world of darkness. The first task of every Christian is to be like Jesus. We are to give ourselves wholly to the pursuit of being like Christ. We must never urge in public what our private lives do not display. It needs to be said over and again.

The dove is God's messenger, and the symbol of peace sent to us through the Holy Spirit.

In Genesis 8: 6–12, we read:

> After forty days Noah opened the window he made in the ark and sent out a raven, and it kept flying back and forth until the water had dried up from the earth. Then he sent out a dove to see if the water had receded from the surface of the ground. But the dove could find no place to set its feet because there was water over all the surface of the earth; so it returned to Noah in the ark. He waited seven more days and again sent out the dove from the ark. When the dove returned to him in the evening, there in its beak was a freshly picked olive leaf! Then Noah knew that the water had receded from the earth. He waited seven more days and send the dove out again, but this time it did not return to him.

I will admit that I have always been fascinated by the cooing of the turtle dove, and I will never forget the sadness that it displays. This very sweet sound from this bird of sorrow comesacross as a symbol of the Holy Spirit, a symbol that we find in the scriptures alluding to the mourning dove. You ask, "Of the Holy Spirit, how can this be true?" I say, "Because love is always sensitive to suffering."

It is true that the Holy Spirit is known for loving, even when He is in deep sorrow. We never read of the anger of the Holy Spirit, but of the grief of the Spirit. In the Book of James, we read: "The Spirit that dwells in us loves us to jealousy." Of course, one of our favorite symbolisms of the dove is peace. The dove from the ark was a messenger of peace, as is the Holy Spirit a messenger of peace with God through the Lord Jesus Christ. Yes, the Holy Spirit leads the soul to accept the message of mercy and to find the peace of God and the deeper peace of God, which keeps the heart and mind in Christ. Where the Holy Spirit rules, there is peace.

In addition to the dove and its symbolism of peace, we have the raven—a black bird—symbolizing darkness. The raven fluttered around here and there, exhibiting a spirit of the troubled spirit of evil. It finds no rest, even in sinful pleasures. It hops and flutters around from sin to sin and finds no peaceful rest until it is finally lost unto eternal condemnation. As we all know, the Holy Spirit keeps us at rest in His bosom of peace—"The peace that passeth all understanding!"

Let us also see the dove as a symbol of purity. You have heard the saying, "As harmless as a dove." The Holy Spirit, the dove of the purity, cannot live in a sinful heart or in a filthy mind. It is like a beautiful flower growing out of a compost garden, and yet as spotless as the wings of an angel. Having the purity of the Holy Spirit within us, we may be surrounded on all sides by corruption and evils of all kinds, and yet come out unaffected and unsullied by the filthy environment. We come out untouched by the evil one!

Dear reader, with the Holy Spirit living within you, your life will be characterized by gentleness, meekness, kindness, and Christ-like love, all of which are "the fruits of the Spirit."

God's Covenant, through the in-dwelling Holy Spirit, shall abide within us into eternity.

Now, let us examine the presence of the Holy Spirit from another point of view. We noted that the dove, having left the ark and returned with an olive leaf in its beak, symbolized the peace and the forgiveness of God that was to come to the earth and proceed to the resurrection of Jesus Christ. Yes, the Holy Spirit had come to the earth to dwell among men.

Here we find the Holy Spirit is in Christ. Jesus said that He was *with* the disciples, but He added that He shall be *in* you. In other words, the Holy Spirit dwelt in Jesus and touched the hearts of men from time to time.

Now, as Paul Harvey would say, "Here is the rest of the story." Jesus at Pentecost placed the Holy Spirit *in* believers, and His home is now in you and me, in the hearts of all believing Christians, and in the Body of the Church. This earth is His home, and here among sinful, suffering mankind, He is preparing us for the eternal kingdom, where we shall one day offer up our praises face-to-face to the Almighty God.

In Genesis 9:12–17, God said:

> "This is the sign of the Covenant I am making between me and you, and every living creature with you, a covenant for all generations to come: I have set my rainbow in the clouds, and it will be the sign of the covenant between me and the earth. Whenever I bring clouds over the earth and the rainbow appears in the clouds, I will remember my covenant between me and you and all living creatures of every kind. Never again will the waters become a flood to destroy all life. Whenever a rainbow appears in the clouds, I will see it and remember the everlasting covenant between me and all living creatures of every kind upon the earth." So God said to Noah, "This is the sign of the covenant I have established between me and all life on the earth."

I heard my mother singing these words all the time:

> When Jesus went down to the waters that day,
> He was baptized in the usual way,

When it was done, God Blessed His Son,
He sent down His love, on the wings of a dove.
(From the hymn "Wings of a Dove")

God's in-dwelling Holy Spirit provides the wisdom needed to witness to our loving relationship with Jesus Christ.

Finally, I think we should place Noah in Faiths Hall of Fame; he pleased God and walked with Him. In other words, his life was focused on God—he walked with Him, had an enjoyable relationship with Him, and pleased Him. He was devoted to God, and this is what is meant by godliness.

Yes, faith in God strengthens the power of the Holy Spirit, and it is that power that provides the wisdom to remain devoted to God. This deep and sincere devotion leads to "devotion in action," which is more than just a warm, emotional feeling about God and is much more than just singing hymns, studying the scriptures, or spending time in prayer. They are important, but devotion is more than mere activities; it is an attitude toward God. It is an attitude that displays His spiritual wisdom in our lives, and it provides the opportunity for us to "walk in His light" through this world of darkness.

We have just read where "God sent down His love on the wings of a dove"—the dove is a symbol of the Holy Spirit. We are supposed to be the light of the world, and this can only happen through the power of the Holy Spirit within us. This is what is meant by the light of Christ in our lives. Since we have "put on Christ" as a new identity, we are bound to live worthy lives, and our actions should bear witness to our union with Christ. His presence should be manifested in us and through us.

My dear Christian friend, if we are called by God to live in holiness and if we find it beyond our power to do so, then it only makes sense that God Himself must give us the light, the strength, and the courage to fulfill the task He requires of us.

I will close by referring back to Noah and the dove as a symbol of the Holy Spirit within us. If we do not shine His light in this world of darkness, it is simply because we do not allow ourselves to avail of the power given to us by God Himself.

> My Savior, thou has offered rest—
> Oh, give it then to me,
> The rest of ceasing from myself,
> To find myself in Thee.
> Amen

Abraham

Abrum—"The Exalted Father"
Abraham—"The Father of Many"

The Lord said to Abraham, "Leave your country, your people, and your father's household and go to the land I will show you. I will make you a great nation, and I will bless you; I will make your name great, and you will be a blessing; I will bless those who bless you, and whoever curses you I will curse; and all peoples on earth will be blessed through you."

Yes, this covenant that God made with Abrum is still in effect some three thousand years later. Through Abrum's family tree, Jesus Christ was born to save humanity. It is through Jesus Christ that you and I can have a personal relationship with God and can be blessed right into eternity! God only asked for one thing—that Abrum leave his home and family and travel to a new land where God promises to build a great nation from Abrum's family. Abrum obeyed, walking away from his home for God's promise of greater blessings in the future.

And now, dear reader, I ask you to give this some thought. Perhaps, God is trying to lead you to a place of greater service and usefulness to Him. Do not let the comfort and security of your present position cause you to miss God's plan for you. I can speak to this point on a very personal basis. I was well-established in a teaching career. The subject was American History, and I was teaching it at the eighth grade level. In December on my fifth year of teaching, the pastor of our church came to school to talk to me. He asked me if I would be willing to go to Ghana, British West Africa to manage two hospitals, 125 miles apart. One was in Adidome, and the other was in Wora Wora. This was only to be for a short time until they could find two career missionaries to take my place. We talked to the superintendent, Mr. Harold Cook, who told me to go ahead and that the teaching position would be mine when I returned. This, my friend, was not an easy decision to make. It was, however, somewhat easier than Abrum's, but it did take considerable thought, family discussions, and much deeper heartfelt prayer. I was in Ghana for three years!

However, as you know, Abrum was called out of a culture of idolatry. God was not simply calling him *away* from something damaging, destructive, and sin-laden, but his calling was *into* something new and fresh, not only a new place geographically but new place spiritually.

Often when we are going through a time of God's dealings, times of brokenness and humbling, all we can see is the pain and the change, and sometimes it terrifies us. Just as I was thinking, and Abrum was thinking, "Where are we going?" we are many times going to a place where we've never been before. We are not just being called to take steps *out* of a sinful nature and destructive past; we are being called *into* a new place of liberty, times, and without realizing it, we are walking into finishing the work of our Lord and Savior Jesus Christ.

Wisdom will bear your heart and soul through the Valley of the Shadow of Death until you reach eternity with Him.

God is at work in these scary times of change in our lives. Yes, what an awesome covenant God made with Abrum.

When we look back at fulfillment of all that God promised Abraham, we can see that Jesus Christ was the promise realized in all that His birth, life, death, and resurrection accomplished for our salvation!

The next time you find yourself wondering, "God, what is going on with my life? It feels like everything is coming apart!" trust God through it all. Your faith, by the power of the Holy Spirit, will provide the wisdom to help you see that He is not simply bringing you *out* of something sinful and destructive, but *into* something large and transforming. He is in the process of connecting you, by faith, righteousness, and wisdom, to something important for His Kingdom.

It is so true, believe me, that people in this world today receive good things, heavenly blessings, because Christians are living faithfully on earth. So, we should be encouraged and comforted whenever we see His blessings. It proves to us that the church is still present on earth and that God's people, though small in number, have not disappeared completely. It is for the sake of these Christians that God shows His grace to everyone in the world.

Unbelievers do just the opposite. They think they are responsible for the blessings they receive, attributing all good things to their own wisdom and effort. In their misplaced self-confidence, they indulge in their pleasures, getting drunk and practicing their idolatrous behavior as hopelessly as did the people of Sodom and Gomorrah. In the end, they will receive the punishment they deserve, while God's people will remain securely in His care.

Make no mistake about it; devout Christians will always suffer in this world. Our lives are filled with troubles and travails: "God works for the good of those who love Him, who have been called" (Romans 8:28). Suffering kills the sinful nature and allows the gifts, the many blessings of God, by means of the power of the Holy Spirit and its wisdom, to multiply.

Do you understand the horror of darkness? The soulless life of sin and idolatry? When terrible sorrow, which is so hard to accept alongside our devoted love, crushes down upon us, rendering our hearts and minds useless, unkindness and cruelty beset our souls. It is in these pitiful trials that our faith shines through. It is trust and wisdom that are waiting to bear your heart and soul through the valley of the shadow of death until you finally see the sun shining on the other side. By following the promises and Abraham, you will see the dawn and daylight and witness the soul at rest in the peace of God's Holy Spirit within you.

Dear friend, when troubles are stinging you, when the devil whispers, "God has forgotten you, God has forsaken you," do not succumb to Satan's falsehoods. No, no, only cling to the Lord more faithfully, more tenaciously.

Let us enjoy the light when it is His pleasure to give it to us, not by attaching our lives to His gifts, but to Him alone. Abraham thought of Him alone when he went up to sacrifice his son Isaac in the region of Moriah. He was giving to God his most precious treasure—his beloved son.

Sacrifice, in the Bible, means that we give to God the best we have. It is the very finest form of worship. It is not giving up things, but giving to God with joy the best we have.

We too, like Noah, "can find favor in the eyes of the Lord."

The worldly culture today demotes the idea of surrender and sacrifice. We have taken the life out of those words and made them mean something sad and unworthy and not at all desirable—just the opposite of the scriptural meaning.

When I surrender to God, I am surrendering the miserable sense that I have of my own self-importance. I gladly surrender myself to Him in order to better comprehend the blessings He has in store for me.

Abraham surrendered himself entirely to God. Have you surrendered yourself to God? You will never know what blessings He has in store for you until you surrender your heart, mind, body, and soul to Him. Indeed, your faith, by the means of the power of the Holy Spirit within you, will provide the wisdom to accept His love and His blessings from here right into eternity with Him!

Keep in mind that in verse 3 of chapter 6 in the book of Genesis, God said, "My Spirit will not contend with man forever, for he is mortal; his days shall be one hundred and twenty years." In other words, God was allowing the people of Noah's day 120 years to change their sinful ways.

God shows His great patience with us as well. He is giving us time to quit living our way and begin living His way, the way He shows us in His Word. However, their time ran out, and the flood waters swept across the earth. Your time may also be running out. Turn to God to forgive your sins. You cannot see the stopwatch of God's patience, and there is not bargaining for additional time.

The people's sin grieved God. Our sin breaks God's heart as much as sin did in Noah's day. Noah, however, did please God, although he was far from perfect. We can follow Noah's example and find "favor in the eyes of the Lord" in spite of the world's sins that continue to surround us. Noah was a righteous man; he wholeheartedly loved and obeyed God. Noah walked step-by-step in faith as a living example of the people of his generation.

We too live in a world full of sin and corruption, filled with idolatrous sin and corruption. I ask you, are we influencing others, or are we being influenced by others, by the worldly ones? In the scriptures, there are many examples of covenants that God made with His people. How reassuring it is to know that God's covenant is established with us! He is still our salvation, and we are kept through our deep and heartfelt relationship with Him. We are well aware of the fact that things have not changed all that much since the days of Noah. Thousands of people are warned every day of God's inevitable judgment, yet most of them do not believe in God. He will deny His judgment and will try to get you to deny God as well. But keep in mind that God promised Noah to keep him safe. This inspires us to trust God for deliverance in the judgment that is sure to come.

Abraham did as God asked, Mary and Joseph did the same.

Yes, we have learned that God did show both wrath and compassion to the people of the earth from the very beginning. He evicted Adam and Eve from the Garden of Eden. He evicted Cain from the garden for murder. He brought on the great flood in those very early days of darkness, violence, sin, and corruption. However, He also exhibited compassion to the people. He clothed Adam and Eve before evicting them. He marked Cain for his safety before convicting him. And, of course, He placed Jonah and his family, along with the animals, upon the ark that He instructed Noah to build.

Another fascinating thought—look at the similar ties between Abraham's story and the story of Mary and Joseph. They were also in unknown territory in tier faith. They had no idea of the marvelous plan that God was working on. I can understand how they could have walked away, if for no other reason than for the fear and the misunderstanding that they were facing. Think of the disrupting factors that this move could make in their lives. How were they to know what blessings they were to receive by accepting this call? I felt the same way about going to Africa as a missionary, and now I can tell you it turned to be a wonderful, wonderful blessing in my life. It was by faith alone that Abraham did as God asked. Mary and Joseph accepted His plan through their faith as well.

Now I am asking you, what blessings have you received? Keep them in your heart and store them up where I do—in the deepest recesses of my soul. Yes, think of those blessings often and, in the meantime, draw ever closer to God in your loving, faithful relationship with Him. Think of all of the promises that Abraham received from God. A country, Israel, was named after him and his ancestors, and he would be called great. He would also be blessed (the word *blessed* was used eighty-eight times in the book of Genesis). Try, if you will, to imagine Abraham surrendering to fear and refusing to go when God said, "Go!" He would have lost all of the promises, the blessings, and the salvation.

God planned to develop a nation of people He would call His own. He called Abraham from the godless, self-centered city or Ur to go to Canaan where a God-centered, moral nation could be established. Although a small dimension, the land of Canaan was the focal point for most of the history of Israel and the rise of Christianity. This small land given to one man, Abraham, has had tremendous impact on world history.

At this point, Abraham built an altar to the Lord. Altars were used by many religions, but for God's people, altars were more than places of sacrifice. For them, altars symbolized communion with God and commemorated noble encounters with God. Abraham regularly built altars to God for two reasons—one, for prayer and worship, and two, as reminders of God's promise to bless him. Abraham could not survive spirituality without regularly renewing his love and his loyalty to Almighty God. Building altars helped Abraham to remember that God was at the center of his life. Regular worship helps US to remember what God desires and motivates us to obey Him in all things.

We also are to live in obedience and gratitude to God.

Countless times throughout the scriptures we see God showing His love and patience toward men and women in order to save them. Even though he realizes their hearts are evil, He continues to try to reach them. When we sin, we fall away from God, and we deserve to be destroyed by His judgment. But God has promised never again to destroy everything on earth until the judgment day when Christ returns to destroy evil forever.

I urge you to write these two verses on the tablets of your heart:

- Noah did everything just as God had commanded him.
- Noah found favor in the eyes of the Lord.

The story of Noah's life involves two great floods—the world was "flooded with evil," and God's response was to flood the earth and to have Noah build the ark. This took 125 years. Many of us have trouble sticking to any project, whether it be directed by God or not. This is a tremendous challenge that Noah gives us—that is, to live in acceptance of God's grace through an entire lifetime of obedience and gratitude.

Dear reader, in retrospect, what you have learned up to this point is that God does make promises and that these promises are fulfilled in His time. Interestingly enough, all of this work has come from the halfway point between the creation and the cross. At this point, God moved from dealing with nations to dealing with man through whom He will make a nation, from which will come the Savior, our own Lord Jesus Christ. Yes, God was dealing with nations, but today He deals with individuals.

It is true—Abraham is one of the world's most famous men of all time. He was a kind and generous man. He lived in an earth-changing time. He was a man of destiny. More significantly, however, he was a man of great faith and believed in God; therefore, God declared him to be a righteous man.

Look at it this way: God had been dealing with the entire human race—that is, man, with his pride, sinful mind, lust, and open rebellion against God, God's patience grew thin. God turned then from nations to one individual. The result was a new nation led by one man—Abraham—and from this new nation the world's redeemer arrived.

When God spoke of "all the families on earth," He was introducing us to a great nation—Israel. God told us of His intentions, His gracious divine promises to Abraham, and we can rest assured that all of God's promises will be fulfilled. Oh, yes, we have seen the wrath of God—Adam and Eve rejected from the garden forever, Cain from the garden for murder, and the great flood.

Now let us think upon the blessings that we have received as a result of God's loving compassion. Through the sacrifice of His only Son, we have, through faith, the gift of salvation and eternal life with Him. Yes, Abraham surrendered himself entirely to the loving Father.

Have you surrendered to Christ? Do you have a close personal and loving relationship with God? I urge you now to surrender your whole life to God. Go out of your sinful mind and surrender. Through surrendering, may your deeper faith lead to righteousness, and may wisdom keep you in His arms eternally.

When you deny yourself, and do good works for others, you are living in God's holy wisdom.

Abraham was not promised wealth or fame; he already had that. Instead, God promised him to have descendants numbering like the stars in the sky. This was quite a blessing when you consider the fact that at the time Abraham was doubting he would ever have an heir. And now God is promising descendants too numerous to imagine. God's blessings are beyond man's imaginations. Abraham believed the Lord, and the Lord credited it to him as righteousness. Yes, Abraham said Amen to God. God said, "I'll do things for you," and Abraham said, "I believe you. Amen, I believe it." This is considered holy righteousness.

Remember, my friend, when you do good works for you salvation, you are exemplifying righteousness and demonstrating acts of wisdom. However, you and I both know that God saves only grace, no other way. If you are saved, it is because you believe God. Abraham believed in God. He accepted what God said, and that is how you are saved. You believe that God has done something for you, that Christ died for you and rose again. God will declare you righteous because you accept His Son, Jesus Christ.

John 5:24 says, "I tell you the truth, whoever hears my word and believes Him who sent me has eternal life and will not be condemned. He has crossed over from death to life." If you have faith, you are blessed; along with Abraham, you are righteous. Later in history, God gave the Laws to Moses, and righteousness was acting according to the Law—Abraham's righteousness was faith. Paul said that Abraham was righteous because of his belief, and you and I are Christians through our belief and our faith in Christ. Abraham demonstrated faith through actions, but it was his belief, not his actions, that made him righteous with God. We know God is what He says He is, and He will do what He says He will do; therefore, our sight actions follow naturally.

Our wisdom leads us to these points:

- Abraham lived in a historically momentous time.
- He was a true man of destiny, on the crossroads of time.
- He was a man of faith.
- All of the great men of the world had strong beliefs in something.
- Abraham believed in God.

God had been dealing with the entire human race—man with his pride, sins of the mind, lust, and open rebellion against God. God's patience grew thin.

Methusalah was 969 years of age. God waited until the entire generation passed away before He brought on the great flood. Then God turned from tribes and races to one individual. God brought a new nation, and out of the new nation, God brought a deliverer—one man, Abraham.

The journey of Abraham and his wife Sarah is just like our Christian life. We too are reaching for the promised future. We too shall fall short of final fulfillment in our lifetime. We have had many signs along the way, abundantly blessed, but by our faith we never lose hope, forever looking forward to the "lasting city!"

Yes, dear reader, that eternal realm remains ahead of us until our dying day.

Wisdom: Realizing we trust, not because a god exists, but because our God exists.

Walk with us, Lord and master. Let us feel the touch of your hand, let us hear your voice, your rebuke if need be. Keep us always on the upper track with you. Let our feet be jubilant beside you, and your eyes always upon the goal. Hold us when we stumble, lift us when we fall. Give us the strength to persist. Endow us with your encouraging words of Wisdom. Amen.

Isaac

❦

Isaac remained close to the Lord. Let us follow his example and remain in God's presence at all times. This patriarch, Isaac, has a very fascinating history.

All of us are most familiar with the sacrifice that Isaac's father, Abraham, was to perform at a place called Moriah. God was testing Abraham, and Abraham proved himself to be worthy of God's trust. The choice of the name Isaac (meaning "he laughs") brought back the joyful feeling of receiving their child (Abraham and Sarah), a long-awaited answer to their prayer. It was another testimony to God's power in making His promise a reality.

In a family of outgoing personalities, Isaac was the quiet, deep-thinking, unobtrusive type. He was the protected only child from the time his mother Sarah got rid of Ishmael until Abraham arranged his marriage with Rebekah. Isaac was part of God's plan. The example his father gave him included a great faith in God! God's promise to create a great nation through which He would bless the world was passed on by Isaac through his twin sons. It is true that Isaac had shortcomings, just as we do, but we must understand that God works through people, regardless of their shortcomings, and many times through them as well.

Isaac was a man of prayer. As you pray, put into words your desire to be available to God just as Isaac did. You will discover that His willingness to use you is even greater than your desire to be used. Who could believe that Abraham would have a son at age 100 and live to raise him to adulthood! But doing the impossible is everyday business to God. Our big problems won't seem so impossible if we let God handle them. Isaac thanked God for His goodness and guidance. Our first response to God should be praise and thanksgiving for His choosing to work in and through us.

Genesis 24:12 shows Isaac praying, "O Lord God of my master Abraham, give me success today and show kindness to my master Abraham," and in Genesis 24:63, it is written that Isaac "went out into the field one evening to meditate." Isaac prayed to the Lord on behalf of his wife because she was barren. The Lord answered his prayer, and his wife became pregnant.

As Isaac pleaded with God for children, so the Bible encourages us to ask, and even plead, for our most personal and important requests. God wants to grant our requests, but He wants us to ask Him. Even then, as Isaac learned, God may decide to hold His answer for a while in order to (1) deepen our insight into what we really need, (2) broaden our appreciation for His answers, or (3) allow us to mature so we can use His gifts more wisely.

Dear reader, this brings to mind a great saying of our Lord Jesus: "If you remain in me, and my words remain in you, ask whatever you with and it will be given to you. This is my Father's glory, that you bear much fruit, showing yourself to be my disciples."

Yes, Isaac went out into the field to meditate and to remain close to the Lord. God considers all human thinking, morality, sunlight—even wisdom—to be dim and blurry compared to His Word. His Word is the light of the world. Through teaching, preaching, devotions, and constant prayer, God will no longer be hidden from us.

We would be better Christians if we spent more time alone in a field or wherever we can find solitude for devotion and prayer. We must attempt to do less and to spend more time alone with Him, quietly in His presence. We boast so often of "having all of our irons in the fire," and yet, no time is more profitably spent than the time we set apart for quiet meditation, talking to God, focusing on being with Him. We must make more time to accept the solemn messages that God is pleased to send to us. Let's find time to do nothing, think nothing, plan nothing. Let's spend our time enjoying a loving relationship with the Lord. You say, "Oh, I can't waste the time. I have work to do." I say, "Spending time with Him is not wasted time!" If I wanted to go fishing, would spending time hunting for earthworms be wasted? Or if I stopped to sharpen the mower blades, would that be wasted time?

Let us follow the example of Isaac and get away to be alone for solemn, quiet meditation with God. Let us take time for a walk in the woods, or to stroll on a beach, or to walk through a beautiful rose garden. They will rid your mind and your heart of all of the worldly deceptions and make your heart beat with a new joy and an enlightened hope. Would you agree, my friend, that today's world is overladen with sins of all kinds, with corruption and ungodliness bringing havoc to all corners of the earth? There are hidden sources of destruction that are subduing the young and the elderly, with lying and deception attacking our mental and spiritual stability, causing much grief and the decline of our moral standards. Only God can lift us up and give us the willpower to overcome evil. Let us draw nearer to Him. Let us go to those who have never met our Savior, our Redeemer, and Lord. Young and old are tired of this life; all are desperately seeking change. God is looking down upon us with His precious love. Let us draw near to Him.

Isaac, in his sublime wisdom, found the solution. He knew the value of intercessory prayer—petition, worship, praise, longing, satisfaction, sorrow, and joy—all come from a heart thrown open to God. The better we know Him, the more we want to pray to Him. The more we pray with sincere trusting hearts, the better we know Him.

I had a wonderful Christian friend, Doctor Elmer Whitcomb, a surgeon in our Christian hospitals in Ghana and who was also a saint of God. He was quiet and meek, and prayer was his very life. I saw him bowing in prayer before every surgery, and then I saw him praying as he walked among his patients throughout the hospital. The praying never stopped—they continued quietly within his heart. I observed him living and breathing in God's presence just as our bodies breathe in our fresh air. He was truly a godly man. He told me one time that "troubles will make you either bitter or better. Notice how very much alike these words are and how very little is needed to change them: just the letter I!"

Isaac was a man with a very strong faith in God. He dedicated his life to developing a close and loving relationship with the Father. In Psalm 63:1–4, King David said, "Oh God, you are my God. Earnestly I seek you; my soul thirsts for you…because your love is better than life, my life will glorify you. I will praise you as long as I live, and in your name I will lift up my hands." True devotion to God is not some special grace given to patriarchs such as Isaac. It is adoration, pure and simple. Our adoration soars beyond ritual, beyond discipline, beyond schedules and timetables and appointments with God. It is your soul reaching out and finding out and finding God's heart reaching back.

This will lead you to a strong loving faith, blending in with the power of the Holy Spirit, which is the source of the wisdom that our souls are so graciously seeking.

Dear reader, may I ask, "Are you fulfilled with the Holy Spirit?" Let us pray right now for your fulfillment. Trust Him to fill you, ask Him to fill you, and allow it to happen. May you be filled with the Holy Spirit day by day, and trust the Lord to have His way with you. Yield to Him, especially when you feel that He is telling you that something is not right in your life. Listen to Him always, abide in His Wisdom as you are filled with the Holy Spirit. May the Lord guide and direct you with His Grace as you draw ever nearer to Him. Amen.

Jacob

Jacob was the third in line of God's plan to fulfill His covenant with the Jewish people. In Genesis 28:15, God says, "I am with you and will watch over you wherever you go, and I will bring you back to this land." Genesis 25:8 also says, "Abraham gave up the ghost, and died in a good old age, an old man, and full." Yes, Abraham died full, not of years only, but of life, of experience, of all great things. By faith, he had abandoned much, but he had gained far more. He had come to know God, to walk with Him, to talk with Him, to enter into a true fellowship with Him in all of the great happenings of his heart. He was called "the friend of God" (James 2:23).

Abraham died full, for in his fellowship with God he had learned to measure time by eternity. Such a man's death is but passing on to wait the accomplishments of the purposes of God as well as the promises of God on the other side. The fullness that men, who live by sight and not faith, gain is a fullness of which they are emptied in death. They leave their possessions behind them. The men of faith carry their fullness with them. It is a great thing thus to die full.

God's covenant promise to Abraham and Isaac was offered to Jacob as well. However, it was not enough to be Abraham's grandson. Jacob had to establish his own personal relationship with God. Let's pause here and think of our own relationship with God. God has not grandchildren; each of us must have our own personal relationship with Him. Stories about the wonderful Christians in your family prove very little. You need to become part of the Christian family through your own loving, faithful relationship with God (as in the old story of "being born in a garage doesn't make you an automobile").

Eventually, Jacob was caught up in a deceitful plan by his mother Rebekah. She lured him into stealing his brother Esau's inheritance from his father Isaac. He did acquire the coveted blessing by deception, but it did cost him dearly. His mother had to leave, Esau hated him, and Jacob was separated from his family for many years.

Try, if you will, to just imagine how much better his life would have been if he and his mother had waited for God to work His way and in His own time. The whole story shows how God overrules the blunders of men, but it also shows the folly of wrongdoing and teaches us how human cleverness, acting apart from God's guidance, falls in to the most serious of difficulties. How constantly, when we turn aside from the pathway of simple obedience, we count up the cost and how again and again we have to learn that we were wrong in our disobedience. You and I both know that our cleverness is always at fault when it attempts to arrive at a divine goal in any other way than by traveling along the godly marked pathway. What constant pain should we be spared from if we really believed that God always works for them that wait for Him? This is godly wisdom from His Word.

How different our lives would be if we would only wait for God to work His own way, and in His own time.

Let me assure you, my friend, that when you lose something that you value greatly, or if someone has deceived you and conspires against you, you will lose control of your emotions. However, if you will control yourself, you will see correctly what to do. Pray to God for help and find a way to solve the very difficult situation.

This is what we mean when we encourage others to maintain a constant, loving relationship with God. Keep a strong and faithful heart and allow the Holy Spirit to take control of your emotions; in other words, allow God's wisdom to rescue you from a seemingly impossible situation.

I feel that this particular historical event in the Bible can be a powerful source of improvement in our lives today. When Jacob's wife learned that her father-in-law was preparing to give his blessing to Jacob's older brother, Esau, she came up with a plan to get the blessing of Jacob. She planned something wrong to accomplish a cruel and deceptive act. She thought, as many of us do in sinful situations, "the end justifies the means." However, no matter how good we think our goals are, we should never attempt to achieve them by doing what is wrong. Ask yourself, "Would God approve of this method of achieving my goal?"

Through faith and by the power of the Holy Spirit and through a personal relationship with God, we will be supplied with the wisdom to help us react correctly to a situation that is about to expose our deceitful motive. Many times we are more worried about getting caught than about doing what is right. Jacob did not seem to be concerned about the deceitfulness of his mother's act, but he was worried about getting caught. Sound familiar? Let your fear about getting caught be a warning to you to do what is right. Correcting yourself in the middle of wrongdoing may bring hurt and disappointment, but it will more importantly bring freedom from sin's control. Think of it: how different his life would have been had he and his mother waited for God to work His way in His own time?

Jacob's uncle, Laban, deceived Jacob most cruelly in a marriage situation. Jacob thought he was receiving the hand of Rachel, but Laban substituted Leah secretly. Laban was very deceptive, and every time he offered Jacob something, he had an ulterior motive, which was exceedingly selfish. The name of Jacob has become almost the synonym for cleverness, and there is a great deal of justification for that fact. But Jacob was always honorable in his dealing with Laban. He broke no contracts and fulfilled his obligations.

This is a story to which one's mind constantly recurs when one hears people speaking contemptuously of the Hebrew people. It is a fact that they have outwitted, and still even today are outwitting, many of those who would oppress them. However, for every Jacob among them, we find a Laban accused of deceit. I believe it was because of the Labans that the Jacobs are so crafty. I am sincerely convinced that those who have treated the Jews with justice and consideration have found in them a response of fidelity and faithfulness, which has been irreproachable!

Live for others that you may mature spiritually, and grow in God's Holy Wisdom.

Jacob's faith grew stronger as he gained experience and developed neighborly as well as good family relationships, and as he drew nearer to God. He made it a habit to do more than was expected of him. He worked hard, even after losing many earthly assets. His diligence eventually paid off, and his flocks once again began to multiply.

The lesson for you and me: making a habit of doing more than is expected of us will pay off. First and foremost, it pleases God. Also, it can earn advancement and recognition, enhance your reputation, give you more experience and knowledge, and, finally, help you to develop your spirituality! This is wisdom in action.

It is written in Genesis 32:24: "Jacob was left alone and a man wrestled with him till daybreak. When the man saw that he could not overpower Jacob, he said, 'Let me go, for it is daybreak.' Jacob replied, 'I will not let you go unless you bless me.' The man asked, 'What is your name?' 'Jacob,' he answered." The man said, 'Your name will no longer be Jacob, but Israel, because you have struggled with God and with men and have overcome.'" Jacob had continued the wrestling match all night just to be blessed. He was persistent. God encourages persistence in all areas of our lives, including the spiritual. Where in your spiritual life do you need more persistence? Strong character will develop as you struggle through tough conditions.

This is what Jacob discovered on that night, and it was this discovery that made the Lord victorious. Jacob had contended with men and had prevailed. That has been story all through his life, and the effect of his successes upon his character had been that of making him self-reliant. He remembered, as we also must remember, that these very successes had resulted from the fact that all his life had been arranged and ruled by God.

That was the lesson he had to learn in order that he might be delivered from self-sufficiency, which would inevitably have ruined him. That explains the entire story of him and the secret of his strength. Defeated him that he might find victory! His cry, "I will not let Thee go except Thou Bless me," was not the cry of a man compelling a reluctant God to yield to him, but the sobbing cry of a man casting himself at last at the feet of God, seeking to be healed. From that day forward, he had a limp, and that limp was a sign of his nobility no matter what others thought of it. Jacob knew it was the sign of God's victory—that he was a man ruled by God.

Dear reader, never forget that the fundamental lesson of all true life is that we must be ruled by God. However, there is another lesson to be learned—it is only possible for us to walk if we are accompanied by His rule and His divine strength. Yielding to God is far more than an act; it is an attitude. This attitude of yielding can only be maintained by depending constantly and entirely upon God.

Yes, my dear friend, happy indeed is the soul who is completely at the end of all self-confidence. Then, and only then, is the man safe who can pray: "Grant me now my soul's petition, none of self and all of Thee."

This is wisdom direct from God's Holy Word.

AMEN

Joseph

This is the life story of a true patriarch—a magnificent man of God, fully righteous and blessed with eternal wisdom.

It seems to me that in every sermon, every Sunday school class, every Bible study that I have witnessed, Joseph's story is the most exciting, the most praise-worthy, and the most spiritual. It creates the deepest feelings of purity, righteousness, and wisdom of all of the patriarchs of the Old Testament.

When you read the book of Genesis in one sitting, you cannot help but notice a change in the way God related to His people. At first, He stayed close by, walking in the Garden with them, punishing their individual sins, speaking directly to them, and intervening constantly. Even in Abraham's day, He sent angels with messages for His people.

By Jacob's time, however, the messages were far more vague: a mysterious dream about a ladder, a late-night wrestling match. And toward the end of Genesis, a man named Joseph received guidance in the most unexpected ways.

Genesis slows down when it gets to Joseph, and it shows God working mostly behind the scenes. God spoke to Joseph, not through angels, but through such means as the dreams of a despotic Egyptian pharaoh. If anyone ever had a good reason to be disappointed in God, it was Joseph, whose brave attempts at goodness brought him nothing but trouble. He interpreted a dream to his brothers, and they threw him in a cistern. He resisted a sexual advance, and landed in an Egyptian prison. There, he interpreted another dream to save a cell mate's life, and the cell mate promptly forgot about him.

Don't you sometimes wonder, as Joseph languished for his virtues in an Egyptian prison, did he ask himself questions like: Is God unfair? Is God silent? Is God hidden? Did these questions ever occur to him? And yet, we begin to view it from the angle of God the Parent.

Was God deliberately "restraining His authority" in order to allow Joseph's faith to grow and to mature? Perhaps, this is why Genesis gives more space to Joseph's life than to any of the other patriarchs!

Through his many trials, Joseph learned to trust and to wait. Not that God would prevent hardship, but that He would bless even the hardship. Genesis 50:20 shows that Joseph, choking back tears, tried to explain his faith to his murderous brothers: "You intended to harm me, but God intended it for good!" In the life of this patriarch, we see numerous examples of God's redeeming love. Joseph, by his strong faith, his ever-lasting relationship with God, his inner spiritual strength, brought true wisdom into the forefront of every divine deliberation he had to make.

Joseph, one of Jacob's twelve sons, was obviously the favorite. Hated for this by his brothers, Joseph was sold by his brothers to slave traders only to emerge several years later as a ruler of all of Egypt. It is through Joseph's years in Egypt that we shall learn how suffering, no matter how unfair, develops strong character and true godly wisdom.

Those who remain close to God, ready and prepared to share your God given Wisdom.

Ancient Egypt was a land of great contrasts. People were either rich beyond measure or poverty-stricken. There wasn't much middle ground. Joseph found himself serving Potiphar, a rich officer in Pharaoh's service.

Potiphar's wife failed to seduce Joseph, who rejected this temptation by saying it would be a sin against God. Joseph refused her advances. Falsely accused of sexual advances, Joseph was put in prison to await his trial. He was in prison for two years until he appeared before Pharaoh, and then he was called out to interpret a dream, not to stand trial.

Dear reader, let us pause here for a moment to consider this stage of Joseph's life. There are some events that can be compared to this life of ours. Our most important opportunities may come when we least expect them. Joseph was brought hastily from the dungeon and pushed before the pharaoh. Did he have the time to prepare? Absolutely not.

He had no warning that he would be pulled from the prison and questioned by the king. And yet, Joseph was ready for almost anything because of his right relationship with God. It was not Joseph's knowledge of dreams that helped him to interpret their meaning; it was his knowledge of God!

Be ready for opportunities by staying close to God. When God calls you to a task, you will be ready with your God-given wisdom. Joseph made sure that he always gave the credit to God, and we should also always do the same—always giving God the glory.

Please, ponder this point as well: when God lets us go to prison because we have been serving Him, and He goes there with us, prison is about the most blessed place in the world that we could be in. Joseph appears to have known that. He did not sulk and groan, nor was he discouraged and rebellious at "everything being against him." If he had, the prison keeper would never have trusted Him. Joseph did not show any signs of self-pity. We should realize that if self-pity is allowed to set in, that will be the end of us, until we fully unload it. Joseph turned everything over in joyous trust to God, and, as a result, the pharaoh turned everything over to Joseph.

> Have you noticed how the geese fly over in the flocks,
> And the way the wolves congregate in packs,
> Or the young Big Horn sheep assemble amid rocks,
> With the older rams protecting their backs?

And yet, the eagle soars alone in the open air,
Daringly dauntless throughout the day,
While the lion lurks in the quiet solitaire,
Stealthily stalking its fearful prey,
You see, strength is not found in bluster and noise,
Not in swaggering, nor through stormy commotions,
Power is demonstrated by the persistence and poise,
Through courage and dutiful devotion.

—Russell Young

We must learn to love the darkness of sorrow; it is there that we will see the brightness of His face. Strength comes from knowing and following Christ. Courage takes us down the path of God's holy righteousness.

Avoid self-centeredness and conceit, remain strong in your soul by living in God's gracious wisdom.

Genesis 43:30 says, "And Joseph made haste for his heart yearned for his brother." This is a touching scene, and it gives us another revelation of how Joseph had been strengthened by his close relationship with God through years of trying experiences. When at last his brother Benjamin was before him, all of the past memories moved his heart to its very limits. Most of us, at one time or another, have found that natural affections have been devastated by adversity, or even by prosperity.

Joseph had passed through suffering that could have hardened his heart and made him forget past associations no matter how scared he was. Not so with Joseph. Yes, he had been through long years of suffering, and he held the highest place of authority in all of Egypt, yet his heart was true to his brother.

This is the way it always is to those who live in a close relationship with God. To the truly righteous among us, we find no bitterness, no arrogance, no self-centered conceit. The heart remains young and tender, and the soul is strong. Joseph's love for Benjamin was natural, but it remained strong by his loyalty to Almighty God.

Each one of us must learn in God's School of Difficulty and Hardship; our wisdom shall teach us to say, "Blessed is the night, for it reveals to us the stars," and we can exclaim, "Blessed is sorrow, for it reveals God's Comfort!"

I read recently of a man whose home and his workshop were washed away in a flood. He stood by the receding waters, all broken-hearted and defeated. Then, he saw something shining on the bank, which had caused his financial ruin—it had made him rich. This is what happened to Joseph, and it is still happening in many lives today. Joseph's faith was given time to grow and mature. In the meantime, he simply had to suffer, to accept the difficult times, and to just "hang in there." He felt like he was dying, but his groaning didn't cause any real harm.

God will remain faithful. Do not despair. Remember what David said in Psalm 27:14: "Wait for the Lord; be strong and take heart and Wait for the Lord!" The Lord will never extinguish that brightly glowing light that continues to shine within your soul. God wants to give us more than we ask for, not just fulfill our weak and insignificant prayers. Joseph asked for nothing more than to be rescued, released from prison, and returned to his father. God heard him pray for that for a long time. God does not usually answer our prayers exactly in the way we ask for them.

For instance, in Ephesians 3:20, we read, "I will give you more than all you ask for or imagine!" That is why you must wait a little longer. We have seen that Joseph did receive what he could never have imagined. He would never have had the confidence or the courage to ask for it. However, we must recognize that God's wisdom, His grace, His mercy, and His power are definitely with us, just as they were with Joseph.

People who live close to God will not demonstrate egotistical attitudes, nor live in a deceptive dishonest way.

Dear reader, can you identify with one or more of Joseph's hardships? He was betrayed and deserted by his brothers, was exposed to sexual temptations, was punished for doing the right thing, endured a lengthy imprisonment, and was forgotten by those he had helped. Now, I ask you, what did Joseph do in each case? His positive response transformed each setback into a step forward! He did not spend time asking, "Why?" His approach was, "What shall I do now?" Those who met Joseph were aware that wherever he went and whatever he did, God was with him.

When you are facing a setback, remember the Joseph-like attitude and acknowledge that God is with you. There is nothing like His presence to shed light on a difficult situation. Notice in Genesis 39:1–2: "And Joseph was brought down to Egypt…And God was with Joseph." In other words, this shows us the relationship is already established, that being brought to Egypt was no accident. In Joseph's life, it is well-demonstrated how true it is that people who live in a close relationship with God do not allow adversities to bring destructive bitterness into their lives. You will see not prideful arrogance or any cruel deceitfulness.

Their divine relationship with God keeps the heart young and tender and the beautiful sights in the soul strong and healthy. Joseph's love for all beings was steadfastly maintained by his loyalty to God. In Genesis 45:5, we read, "God did send me before you to preserve life." Thus, Joseph spoke to his brothers, not just to forgive them for their murderous deeds, but merely to put them at ease before him. It did show them that God had overruled their evil deeds and that God had completed His work through them as His chosen instruments. Thereby, Joseph gave his brothers his loving forgiveness.

We too can do the same for others when we maintain our loyalty to God amid circumstances of trials and suffering. Faith looks up and believes in God regardless of the pain and sees that God's purpose will always be realized. We can all now see that the day will come when we will finally realize the reason for our struggles and trials of life. We will joyfully sing, "Right Is the Pathway to God!" We will one day understand clearly that God has ordered our every step, and our faith will make all things evident. This is a most beautiful illustration of the ways of God. God is infinite in His patience with His own. In hours of special needs, God comes to us and makes Himself known once again for our strengthening and our renewal.

In Genesis 55:25, Joseph says, "God will surely visit you, and you shall carry up my bones from here." Joseph knew that God would come to them when both he and the pharaoh had passed on and that God would come to them when both he and the pharaoh had passed on and that God would bring them into the land He had promised to Abraham, to Isaac, and to Jacob. No matter what difficulties lay ahead, there could be but one final result—the accomplishment of God's holy purpose, the fulfillment of the divine promise!

Thus, in the words of his true faith, ended the life of one of the greatest men in the entire Old Testament. Let us agree—in many respects, Joseph is the most wonderful image of the coming son and servant of God to be found in Israel's profound history. So, Pharaoh asked, "Can we find anyone like this man, one in whom is the Spirit of God?" (Genesis 41:38).

Remember in the good times, as in the difficult times, God is completing His great and glorious goal.

Joseph always made sure that he gave the credit to God.

We should be careful to do the same. To take the honor for ourselves is a form of stealing God's honor. Do not be silent when you know you should be giving the honor to Him. Glorify Him in all that you say and do. In this way, we maintain our loving relationship with Him and, thereby, gain the eternal wisdom of His precious love.

Dear reader, we must try to understand that it was not by accident that Joseph was made captive by his brothers and sold into slavery in a foreign land. God saw the need of thousands of people, and He met that need through the soul of one person—Joseph. Through all of those weary years in prison spent by Joseph alone, God was actively working toward His great and glorious goal. Yes, God saw the pain and suffering of His servant Joseph, but He was looking forward to the final goal. And then, the day came when God brought His servant forth, and his days of suffering were over.

His trust in God became a true blessing. Yes, my friend, it was God that had sent Joseph into bondage. God meant it for good, and there was no other reason for those long years of suffering. Always remember, God's love permits our suffering and difficult afflictions of all kinds, but His ever-loving hands are guiding us through it all. When you feel it is hopeless, just take His hand and follow Him fearlessly. When you reach eternity and look directly into His loving face, you'll see the hands that you trusted, and His Eternal love will be yours to enjoy forever.

Amen.

Rest in Him

Restlessness comes upon us,
    Amidst days of stress, and strife,
It is not our choice to incur it,
    It leads to an unsettled life.
We must step back, slow ourselves down,
    Take a break, give ourselves time to pause,
For restlessness, just as all other ailments,
    Can be traced to a definite cause.

Restlessness comes upon us for a reason,
    The problems can be found far and wide,
The heartaches and headaches stem from
    Our selfishness, ambition, and pride!

Rest can be achieved by yielding,
    You see, it can also be found to have cause,
A heart set deep in God's teachings
    Will find rest in His biblical laws.
Live by and adhere to your convictions,
    Make readiness and love your goal,
Find eternal calm in your strong faith,
    Let peace and poise claim your soul.

> Rest is yours as you lean on your Savior,
> > Peace and contentment flow from above,
> Embrace life with pleasure and gladness,
> > Render service, forgiveness, and love.

> —Russell Young

Dear reader, will you join me here and say, "I love my Master, I will not go free. I will serve Him forever!" Wisdom declares that it is true—God provides the grace to live by, and it is found in His Holy Word.

Heavenly Father, this life is for you. It was never meant to be any other way. I am surrendering it entirely to you. I surrender all that I have since I became yours. I will serve you forever. I will never go free.

Amen.

Moses

God rescued Israel through the patriarch Moses and through many magnificent miracles. We read in the last chapter that Joseph brought his family to Egypt and protected them there. But after Joseph's death, as they multiplied into a nation, they were force into slavery.

God then called on Moses to free His people from slavery and to lead them out of Egypt. Just as God delivered Israel from Egypt, He delivers us from sin and death. Although God is all powerful and can perform miracles, He leads out of sin and into salvation through His Word, from which we gain the wisdom to make daily decisions that rule our personal lives.

The new nation, formed through the covenant with Abraham and his descendants, had the same problems facing Christians today. We are often discouraged, sometimes rebellious, and even sometimes victorious. Our divine guide, however, is still in the wisdom of His holy Word! It was through a series of strange events that a Hebrew boy by the name of Moses became a Prince in Pharaoh's house and then an outcast in a desert land. God visited Moses, and after considerable persuasion, Moses agreed to return to Egypt and to lead God's people out of Egypt.

Yes, my dear friend, God did, through Moses, lead Israel, and He wants to lead us as well. I ask you now—is He leading you to perform a piece of work for Him? He will be with you, so obey and follow Him. Trust Him. Do as He says. Study and obey His holy Word. Recognize and enjoy His presence in your life. Exodus 3:7 says, the Lord said to Moses, "I have seen the misery of my people in Egypt…So now, go. I am sending you to Pharaoh to bring my people out of Egypt." In Exodus 4:13, Moses said, "O Lord, please send someone else to do it."

Let us pause here and collect our thoughts concerning Moses's attitude. He made excuses because he felt inadequate for the task that God asked him to perform. Just a few years ago, I was asked to teach a Sunday school class of people my own age—senior citizens. I was frightened out of my wits to attempt such a thing. I had never taught a Sunday school class before in my life. I was scared to death. However, after talking with the Lord in prayer, seriously discussing my inadequacies, I did finally get up the courage to go for it. It was honestly one of the most joyful years of teaching those wonderful Christian friends.

Moses's reluctance and fear, just like mine, were caused by over anticipation. He was worried about how the people might respond to him. We often build up events in our minds and panic about what might go wrong. God does not ask us to go where He has not provided the means to help. Go where He leads, trust Him to supply courage, confidence, and resources at the right moment. If you really want to be ineffective, start running scared. Think about every peril, focus on the dangers, worry about the what-ifs, and say yes to caution. Expect the worst. Let fear overwhelm you. You are now successful, totally ineffective.

My dear friend, we are all often faced with great opportunities, brilliantly disguised as impossible situations.

Place your trust in God. Your Righteousness will bring His blessings.

Is there something that you know that God expects of you, but you are afraid you will mess it up? Put fear in its place. Let God decide what your capabilities are.

In Exodus 14:13–14, Moses said to the people, "Do not be afraid. Stand firm and you will see the deliverance that the Lord will bring you today. Those Egyptians that you see now; you will never see again. The Lord will fight for you; you need only to be still." One of the most challenging frustrations of leadership is realizing that those who follow do not necessarily see things the way you do. With the Egyptian army on one side and the waves slapping at the other side, the Israelites saw a dead-end. But Moses, in God's Word, saw a clear path to deliverance.

When others do not share your enthusiasm or you willingness to sacrifice for a thing or something that cannot be seen as an uncertain goal, do what Moses did. Tell them what you have learned as clearly and as positively as you possibly can. Then, trust God to bring His result to pass. With the Lord, your righteousness promotes God's blessed assurance through the wisdom of His Word.

Let us emphasize what God said to Moses.

> DESPAIR—says, "Give up," but God says, "Have courage." Always rejoice in His love and His faithfulness.

> COWARDICE—says, "Give up on your Christian beliefs."

> FAITH—hears God say, "Stand firm, keep the Holy Spirit alive within you ready for action, cheerfully and patiently waiting for His voice. It shall not be long before God shall say to you, as clearly as God said to the people of Israel, "Go forward!"

Courage would not be courage if it always came easily. Be willing to stand alone, even when everyone else has given up. That, my friend, is the defining mark of Christian leadership!

Exodus 18:1–3 says, "Now, Jethro, Priest of Midian and the father-in-law of Moses, heard of everything that God had done for Moses and for the people of Israel, and how God had brought His people out of Egypt." Jethro met God through Moses, and Moses received hospitality, his wife, and his wisdom from Jethro. Jethro gave Moses advice, saying, "Listen to me, and I will give you some advice, and may God be with you. You must be the people's representative before God and bring their disputes to Him."

These words make it absolutely clear that Moses had great respect for his father-in-law. Although Moses had not asked for it, he seemed to be sincerely happy to have Jethro's advice.

I do believe you are aware that words of advice can come from people you do not respect, do not like, whose opinions are not welcome. But your character comes through when you can see past the messenger and find hidden value in the message.

Hard lessons can often be the best ones. My high school football coach, Lyle Barber, explained to us that one of the greatest obstacles to growth might not be ignorance; it could be knowledge. He said the more we learn, the greater the chance that we'll think we know it all. When that happens, we become unteachable, and we are no longer growing or improving. He said that if you are to reach your potential, you have to keep growing. When you remain teachable, your potential is almost limitless. True, that year we were not only undefeated, but also not scored upon in the Western Buckeye League football season.

We are welcome to approach God because Jesus has opened the door for us.

Remember, no matter where you are, no matter what you have achieved, no matter how much you know, there is always someone you can learn from. Never get too big for a little advice.

Verse 25 says, "So Moses went down to the people and told them!" Because God's glory and power were so strong, and because God is completely holy, the people could not come to Him. God did this to show He was not like the idols of Egypt that could be seen and touched. Now, however, we are invited to approach God because Jesus opens the way for us to come to God with great joy! The wisdom in the Word leads us directly into His Almighty presence.

Exodus 20:2–3 says, "I am the Lord your God, who brought you out of Egypt, out of the land of slavery. You shall have no other gods before me." These words introduce us to the Ten Commandments. These commandments were given in regard to their daily conduct, their relationships with others, as well as their worship. Let us always remember: these Laws were for His people who had been rescued from slavery in Egypt. Each of the Ten Commandments had to do with their relationship with Him.

He did not give them to His people while they were slaves, as though their freedom depended upon their obedience. No, God gave them the Laws after they were freed from Egypt, which tells us that the Laws are an expression of His love. This is God's way. Recognize them as an expression of His grace. God still gives us conditions by which we direct our conduct and our worship. However, it is in Christ Jesus that grace has its perfect expression, and it is through Him that it is most powerfully demonstrated. And the most strengthening and most comforting thought for us is the fact that every requirement of the Law is rooted in His love.

Let us again look at the opening statement of the Ten Commandments: why did God say, "I am the Lord your God…you shall have no other gods before me." Why does He still challenge us with those words when we want to make our gods of wood and stone? Of silver and gold? Of fame and fortune?

The reason is there are no other gods; we are fooling ourselves. We can give ourselves to them, but they cannot give themselves to us. Many people must come to the point where they discover that the gods of the world are no gods. They pinned their hope on something, gave themselves to it with the same energy as they would in worship, but it has let them down. That is how it is with the gods of the world.

My dear friend, do you look to the Lord who promises to be your inheritance, your Savior, and see Him as sufficient? Or do you sometimes look to other gods?

Sin leads to punishment. Its obedience and repentance that leads to God's healing touch.

Please, dear reader, let this truth sink deeply into your soul—there are no other gods! Numbers 21:6–9 says, "The people in the wilderness grew impatient, and spoke against

God and Moses. Then the Lord sent venomous snakes among them; they bit the people and many Israelites died. The people came to Moses and said, 'We sinned when we spoke against the Lord and against you. Pray the Lord will take the snakes away from us.' So Moses prayed for the people. The Lord said to Moses, 'Make a snake and put it on a pole; then when anyone is bitten by a snake, and looks at the bronze snake, he will live.'"

You and I both know that there was no healing power emanating from the bronze snake. It was simply the result of the obedience they gave to God's order. It touched on of the deepest facts of life—sin and rebellion against the Lord results in divine punishment. They were suffering due to their sin. For healing, they were to bow to God's command and, thus, make it possible for God to restore them and heal them. The principle is obvious—rebellion always results in suffering and disaster. Repentance and returning to God lead to healing.

Thus, we see how the conformation of God's righteousness is in the giving of His mercy. This is similar to our salvation through Christ. We can only receive His atonement by returning to Him in heartfelt repentance and through our abiding faith in Him. That simply means we must commit ourselves fully to Him and continue to enjoy a close, loving relationship with Him at all times. And so, by grace, He has given us a path back to Him, and once again we receive our healing. This is the basis of our human action and the very essence of our God-given wisdom. They had been traveling over the desert without water in sight, famished with thirst. Moses said, "Gather the people together, and I will give them water."

They gathered in circles on the sand. They took their staves and dug deep down into the burning earth, and as they dug, they sang "Spring up, O well, sing ye unto it." There came a gurgling sound, a rush of water, and a flowing stream which filled the well and ran along the ground. When they dug this well in the desert, they touched the stream that was running beneath and reached the flowing water that had never been seen.

This is beautiful, even for us, to meditate upon. It reminds us of the river of blessings that flows all through our lives. All we need do is reach, by faith and praise, to satisfy our thirst for Him in the barren desert of our lives. How did they reach the waters of the well? It was by praise. There is nothing that pleases the Lord as much as praise. There exists a true test of our faith in our offering of grace-filled thanksgiving to the Lord.

Are you praising God enough? Do you regularly thank Him for your blessings? Let us show our love to Him as we walk in His path of righteousness by giving Him our praise and thanksgiving always. This is true wisdom direct from His Holy Word.

Moses was a great prophet. The works of Christ magnifies our sense of greatness of Moses.

> Moses was one hundred and twenty years old when he died, yet his eyes were not weak nor his strength gone. The Israelites grieved for Moses in the plains of Moab for thirty days, until the time of weeping and mourning was over. Now, Joshua, son of Nun, was filled with the Spirit and WISDOM because Moses had laid his hand upon him. So, the Israelites listened to him and did what the Lord had commanded Moses. Since then, no Prophet has risen in Israel like Moses, whom the Lord knew face to face, who did all of those miraculous signs and wonders the Lord sent him to do in Egypt, to Pharaoh, and to all of his officials, and to the whole land. For no one has ever shown the mighty power of performed the awesome deeds that Moses did in the sight of all Israel! (Deuteronomy 34:7–12)

Here we have the story of Moses's death and a tender reference to the greatness of the leader and Law-giver. These words written about Moses remained true all through the history of Israel until one was born of the seed of David who was far greater than Moses. Also, we hear what Moses had foretold: "I will raise them up a Prophet from among their brethren like unto thee."

Yes, dear reader, it is true that many centuries passed by, but at last He came, and in HIS coming, He fulfilled all that Moses had begun under God's rule. He absorbed and abolished the Law that came to Him, along with the grace and truth that He brought to us. The work of Christ does not detract from but enhances our sense of greatness of the patriarch Moses. His passing ceremony was a thing of beauty. The fact that he did not get to lead the Israelites into the Promised Land was God's punishment to him, but, as usual, it was done with God's wonderful mercy. It was magnificent and glorious, ending to a great and significant life.

Perhaps, its greatest value was its revelation of the need for the Redeeming Savior. Through our loving relationship with Almighty God, along with the inner presence of the Holy Spirit, our wisdom shall lead us into eternal life with Him!

> O Father, Self-sufficient as thou art,
> Come to bless my aching heart,
> Hold me in thy precious love.
> O Lord, from thy gracious power Wisdom flows
> Into my life, and heaven knows
> I yearn to be with thee above.
> Amen.

Joshua

Joshua, a magnificent patriarch in his own right, was God's choice to follow His faithful servant Moses in the fulfilling of His covenant of the Promised Land for the people of Israel. Joshua was a brilliant military leader and a strong spiritual influence for God's people. The key to his success was his submission to God. When God spoke, Joshua listened and obeyed. Joshua's obedience served as an example. It was because of Joshua's steadfast faith that Israel remained faithful to God throughout Joshua's lifetime. Joshua proved his faith by taking up the challenge to lead God's people, and people showed their commitment to God by obediently setting out to cross the Jordan River and possess the Promised Land.

As you and I live our Christian lives, we need to cross over from our old lives and step into the new life. We must put off our egotistical, self-centered desires and march off to possess that which God has prepared for us. True, we do need courageous faith to live the new life. Joshua urged the followers to remain in the Lord and to worship Him only. The Israelites had seen God deliver them from many enemies, had seen His miraculous power in providing their needs, but, like many of us, they had a tendency to stray from the Lord. We too have seen God at work in our lives, and we must continually renew our commitment to obey only Him.

Our ability to stay strong in God's work comes from trusting in Him. His promises assure us of His love. By faith, we know He will be with us and support us in the difficulties we face. Faith begins in believing He can be trusted. As long as we maintain our trust in Him and obey His will, He will give us the victory. In Joshua 1:2–3, God said, "Now therefore arise, go over this Jordan, thou, and all this people, unto the land which I do give them......Every place that the sole of your feet shall tread upon, that I have given to you."

Let us all bear in mind that Egypt represents bondage, that the Passover represents salvation through the blood of the Lamb, and that the Red Sea represents the passing from death unto life. It was truly God's intention and His desire to take the children of Israel straight into the Promised Land. It was never His plan that the chosen people should spend forty miserable years as beggars, wandering the wilderness, murmuring, rebelling, fretting, being defeated to the point that the entire generation should end up buried in that sandy desert. Never was that His plan.

It was their own choice not to enter in immediately. It was because of the sin of their unbelief that God's loving work became His punishing work as He sentenced them to forty years in the wilderness. In this way, all people, including you and me, might learn for all time how grievous to the heart of the Lord is the sin of unbelief.

Let's face the facts: it is still God's intention and desire to lead us directly into our inheritance in Christ Jesus. However, just as the children of Israel failed to enter into their inheritance through unbelief and were condemned to those forty years of wandering, it has been the same way with many of us well. It was because of our unbelief in the grace and power of God that we suffer the wilderness experience. We too have a River Jordan to cross, and many of us have not yet crossed it.

Faith convinces us that we are closer to the Lord than we are to ourselves.

Many of us harbor a deep-rooted misconception about faithfulness. We assume that in order to be faithful, we must rid ourselves of doubt and have victory over the struggle. Let's think of the story of Thomas, that disciple whose only claim to fame was that he doubted the resurrection. His very name is used to characterize someone who questions—a Doubting Thomas.

But Thomas wasn't the only one who doubted. He was just honest enough to tell others of his doubts. When Mary Magdalene and the other women came from the tomb on

Easter morning to tell the apostles about the resurrection, "the men did not believe the women, because their words to them seemed like nonsense." Even when Jesus appeared to them, they thought they were seeing a ghost. Still, poor old Thomas gets the brunt of the criticism. But when he finally does see Jesus, he doesn't receive judgment, but acceptance and gentleness and understanding. "Put your finger here," Jesus says, "and see my hands. Reach out your hand and touch my side. Stop doubting and believe." These words do not represent condemnation, but invitation. Thomas spoke his doubts openly, honestly, and Christ answered them. Jesus reached out to him and drew him in.

Faithfulness is not a matter of gritting your teeth and hanging on. It is a matter of trusting the Lord enough to be open about your doubts. It is about having enough faith in God to question. So, go ahead, ask your questions. Your faith will be stronger for it! Faith convinces us that the Lord is nearer to us than we are to ourselves. In what way is God near? Let's just take a step forward to have a look at Psalm 23:4 where David says, "Though I walk through the valley of the shadow of death, I will fear no evil, for you are with me; your rod and your staff, they comfort me."

Even though David could not see or hear the Lord, David said, "Thou art with me." The Lord's presence cannot be perceived by the five senses. Only faith enables us to know that He is there. You ask, "In what way is God near?" He is near to us in His Word. When David said, "Your rod and your staff, they comfort me," it's as if he wanted to say, "Nothing else on earth can help me through my worries and troubles. God's Word alone is my rod and my staff. I will hang on to it and use it to pull myself up again. I will be certain that the Lord is with me and that he gives me courage in all anxieties and troubles. He defies the devil and the world and rescues me from my enemies."

With the words, "Your rod and your staff," David was referring to the image of a shepherd with his sheep. He wanted to say, "A shepherd guides his sheep with his rod and staff and leads them to graze in the meadow and drink fresh water. He also uses his staff to protect them from all dangers. This is the way the Lord, the true Shepherd, leads and guides me with His staff. In other words, He leads me with His Word. Then I can walk with Him on the right path in firm faith and with a clear conscience. I can also protect myself from false doctrine and false piety. Also, the Lord protects me from all spiritual dangers and uses His staff to rescue me from all enemies. God's Word so richly strengthens and comforts me that no spiritual or physical trial is too much to endure or to overcome."

Joshua wants to lead you to the peace that Christ is holding for you.

Today, many miserable, despondent, defeated Christians are standing at the edge of the crossing but have yet to go over completely to Him. Your Joshua—Jesus (symbolism, even the name is the same)—wants to lead you over and invites you to see the power and the peace that await you if you will put your whole trust and your whole faith in Him all the way. Yes, we must see this power. In Joshua 1:5, God said, "There shall not any man be able to stand before thee all the days of your life: As I was with Moses. So shall I be with thee: I will not fail thee, nor forsake thee."

Imagine if you will, their forefathers had stood on the very borders of the Promised Land. Yet, they had failed to enter because they feared the "giants" and the "cities that were walled up to heave." And now, here they are back at the same borders. The giants had not shrunk, the walls were no weaker, but they had the promise—"There shall not any man be able to stand against thee." This time, they believed, they entered, and they possessed. You see, before they entered they had to believe God's promise.

Dear friend, do you believe the promise? If not, you cannot enter. I don't mean we need to be perfect because none of us are. But we must believe His promise as a true believer that "no man will be able to stand against us" in an attempt to cause us to sin. In other words, in our past we have people who treat us like grasshoppers because we had a grasshopper god instead of an Almighty God. Now, as a true believer, not any man shall be able to stand against you because you have begun to trust His Word and His Power, and you now possess the wisdom to overcome sin.

God said to Joshua, "As I was with Moses, so I will be with thee; I will not fail thee nor forsake thee." You might say, "But that promise was given to Joshua, not to me." However, it *was* given to you. This very promise is taken through the Holy Spirit and given to us as it is written in Hebrews 13:5, where we read, "Be content with such things as you have; for the Lord hath said, I will never leave thee, nor forsake thee!"

Now read in Joshua 21:43, "There failed not any good thing which the Lord had spoken unto the house of Israel: All came to pass." Does that put your heart at ease? All of the Lord's promises were fulfilled and are continually being fulfilled, even to this very day. And so in Joshua 1:13, we read, "Remember the command that Moses the servant gave to you: 'The Lord your God is giving you rest, and has granted you this Land!'"

Thus, speaking to the "rest" that we have in the midst of our trials and difficulties, we must fight the good fight of faith as we take our rest and our peace through God's holy power. I have learned that "when a soul learns to trust God for victory over sin and yields itself entirely to God in all of its circumstances and duties and chooses to live only where and how God desires, then that soul enters into rest."

We have learned long ago that a walk for a mile begins with the first step. And so, it is that one step begins and then develops into the long walk of faith, and by continuing on progressively, we receive our inheritance by maintaining an attitude of simple trust in His Word. With presence and the power of God's Holy Word, we will enter into Canaan, the eternal heavens, with the Lord. Yes, this is the wiscom of His precious Word in action.

My Savior, Thou have offered life eternally! Let me enjoy it today, that I may cease from seeking it on my own. I pray to claim it all from Thee.

Amen.

Do others see God reflected in your life? He can make you into another Moses, or another Joshua.

Joshua played an important role in the exit from Egypt. He was the field general of Israel's army and the only one allowed to be with Moses on the pathway up the mountain where Moses received the Law. His basic training was living with Moses, learning firsthand what it meant to lead God's people. This was mentoring at its very best.

And now I ask you to think for a moment: who is your Moses? Who is your Joshua? You are in line to continue God's ongoing work in the world. You are developing yourself after others, and there are others patterning their lives after you. How important is God to those you want to be like? Do those who are watching you see God reflected in every area of your life? You might even want to ask God to lead you to trustworthy Moses, or even ask Him to make you an effective Joshua.

Joshua 21:45 says, "There failed nothing of any good thing which Joshua had spoken unto the house of Israel; all came to pass." The Levites (priests) were devoted and diligent in completing the task pertaining to spiritual things.

They were to live among the people, not separated or isolated from them, but rather to make them witnesses to Israel's relationship with God. They were to make the people aware of the consequences of disobedience to God. Jehovah God gave them the land, and they possessed it. God's every promise to them was fulfilled. Through their obedience to God, no man had been able to stand against them. God delivered their enemies into their hands. Any failure they experienced was wholly due to their disobedience.

As the time for his passing drew nearer, Joshua gathered the people for his farewell address. The final words of this God-centered, truly spiritual patriarch spoke magnificently of the life that we, even today, should write upon the tablets of our hearts. He urgently and earnestly charged the people to maintain a constant loving relationship with God. "Keep yourselves in the love of God." To fail to discipline your life, to stray from God's path of righteousness, is to drift into sin and corruption, resulting in God's fearful punishment.

Finally, he spoke words that are historically significant when he said, "If it seems evil unto you to serve Jehovah, chose you this day whom you will serve." Joshua was saying to his people, and it is still ringing in our ears today, everything of greatness in their history (and ours) is of God! He was saying to them and to us, "Now, therefore, fear God and serve Him! But if not, then choose between the other gods." Yes, what he was saying has great implications on the profound necessity of all human life—man must worship.

He must have a god. That is universally true. So, if men will not serve the Lord, then let them choose whom they will serve, but only let them make their decision with the knowledge that the kingdom of God does mean love, and light, and liberty.

This is our answer to those who refuse our personal appeals today. If they will not have God, tell them they can have their own choice, only let them compare the results of life with Christ, as compared to the life found under any other authority. This is the reason for Joshua's decision, "As for me and my house, we will serve God."

Yes, dear friend and loving Christian, Joshua was a magnificent patriarch and excellent leader and a devoted servant of God. The result of his decision to live out his life in the ever- loving arms of God led him to a great and immeasurable faith and, thus, to unlimited depths of spiritual wisdom.

The Beauty of Jesus

May the love of Christ my Savior,
Live in my heart day by day,
With His Holy power controlling,
Everything I do and say.
May His spirit rest upon me,
As I seek lost souls to win,
By ignoring "self" completely,
May they behold Him.
May my life be a living witness,

To His grace, and His peaceful ways,
That His sacred fire within me,
May burn brightly in all my days.
May the beauty of Jesus be seen in me,
And His Wondrous compassion be mine,
May all of my nature be purified,
By His blessed Spirit Divine!
AMEN

—Russell Young

Prophets

Yes, all of us who have spent time in Bible study or who have read through the Bible have soon learned that prophecy occupies a large space in Scripture. It is a matter of fact that over half of the Bible is devoted to predicting future events. I personally believe that nothing brings greater comfort to a Christian than to understand prophecy. Bible scholars have explained thusly, "No prophecy ever originated because some man made it happen. It never originated in man, but rather man spoke from God as they were moved by the Holy Spirit to do so."

Dear reader, I ask you, what would we get out of our bible reading today if it came solely from the thoughts of men? It would simply be like reading Ernest Hemingway or John Grisham, which after a few years would have lost its flavor and become meaningless to us. But the Holy Bible never loses its meaning since it is a divine revelation. God emerges from Scripture because God originated it. In 2 Peter 1:20–21, it says, "Above all, you must understand that no prophecy of Scripture came about by the prophets own interpretation. Prophecy never had its origin in the will of man, but men spoke from God as they were carried along by the Holy Spirit."

There are a few very basic elements of prophecy that we need to observe. One of the facts is that the prophecy will take place at exactly the right time. Habakkuk 2:3 says, "The revelation awaits an appointed time; it speaks of the end, and it will not prove false." Also, true prophecy is predictive. God told the prophet of things that would happen long before they came to pass. At times, the revelation seems to be delayed, but nothing can stop it from happening.

Dear friend, has God given you a word or promise that has not been completed? Are you wondering if it will ever be done? Has He forgotten His promise? I say to you take heart. He is there for you 24-7. Keep in mind that the majestic God is in control of your life no matter what happens to you.

In 1 Kings 4:32–34, it says, "(Solomon) spoke three thousand proverbs, and his songs numbered a thousand and five. He described plant life, from the cedars of Lebanon to the hyssop that grows out of walls. He also taught about animals and birds, reptiles and fish. Men of all nations came to listen to Solomon's wisdom. Yes, his wisdom came directly from Almighty God as a gift." Read these prophetic words from God to Isaiah in chapter 53, verses 4 to 7:

Surely He took up our infirmities and carried our sorrows, yet we considered Him stricken by God, smitten by Him, and afflicted. But He was pierced for our transgressions, He was crushed for our iniquities; the punishment that brought us peace was upon Him, and by His wounds we are healed. We all, like sheep, have gone astray, each of us have turned to his own way; and the Lord has laid on Him the iniquity of us all. He was oppressed and afflicted, yet He did not open His mouth; He was led like a lamb to the slaughter, and as a sheep before her shearers is silent, so He did not open His mouth. By oppression and judgment He was taken away.

These prophetic words from the prophet Isaiah gave the people a vivid picture of what was to come some several centuries later in their future. We see our Christ despised and rejected by man, bruised and put to horrific grief, and, finally, put to death on the cross. Why? "All we like sheep have gone astray…and God hath laid on Him the iniquity of us all."

Dear reader, with all of my grief and sorrow and shame, I must ask: was it all worth it? Am I worth it? The answer is *yes*, as beautifully drawn out in God's own words—"He shall be satisfied!" Let us all rejoice in our redemption. My friend, God's love is so amazing, so heavenly divine that it demands more than our lives, or even our souls. It demands our all. This, dear reader, is wisdom coming directly from His Holy Word.

Amen.

Samuel/David

Samuel, the twelve-year-old boy, came to be a son of the Law. It was at this time that the Lord spoke to him. He answered the call and committed himself to the will of God. Later, he became an instrument of divine action. Like Moses, Samuel was not only a judge; he was a prophet.

This reveals the attitude of all who are called of God to deliver His word to men. What is that attitude? We must forever be of a wholly-surrendered life and waiting to hear the Word of God. Too many of us fail because we do not listen before we speak. "Wisdom is the reward we get from a lifetime of listening when we'd rather talk." God still waits to speak to those whom He would like to make His desires known. They, in turn, must wait until His message is received.

Has God ever spoken to you? Have you ever listened? It is not that God fails to speak, but that we fail to listen. How long has it been since you quietly waited for God, expecting Him to speak to you? Have you ever done it? Do you really have a sensible, intelligent reason for ignoring the voice of God? I ask you, dear reader, isn't that like refusing to turn on the radio or the TV because you didn't believe that it would produce sound or give a message? Shouldn't you, at least, give it a try first?

Samuel listened. God does speak, is still speaking, has spoken, but we are too busy or too indifferent or too "smart" to listen. Please, my dear friend, take a few minutes to listen to God. You will be surprised, and you will be grateful. This is wisdom in action. During the years that the prophet Samuel passed from youth to manhood, Israel was suffering under oppressive Philistines. The people were moaning and crying after God. Samuel called them to return to Him and to refrain from worshipping idols. Finally, God did intervene, and the powers of the enemy were broken. Samuel built an altar and said, "Hitherto Jehovah helped us." This prophet of clear vision recognized the power of God, along with His merciful purposes and His gracious method of bringing His people back to Him.

Samuel was one of Israel's greatest prophets. He was a man of prayer. He began the school of Prophets, and he Anointed Israel's first Kings. He chose, anointed, and prepared David- Israel's greatest King. However, Israel found out that establishing Kings to rule over them did not solve their problems. If you and I will look back in all honesty, we will see that God has always been acting for our highest good, even though we did suffer difficulties and sorrow. Let us continue to look back and, thereby, see more clearly in the present and give hope with confidence for the future.

As you and I both know, no government or set of Laws can substitute for the rule of God in your heart or in your life. God is always at work in this world, even if we cannot see what He is doing. No matter what kinds of pressure we might feel or what kinds of changes we might endure, God is at work. God is in control of the situation at all times. By being well aware of that fact, we can face difficult situations in our lives with confidence and courage. If you truly desire to be a leader, God must guide every particle of your work—your values, your goals, and even the way you raise your children.

This includes trusting Him in all things and maintaining a strong personal relationship with Him. This will result in a stronger faith, power of the Holy Spirit, and being blessed with the promised wisdom to control your life. God faithfully kept the promise He made to Israel. He gave to His people His tender mercy and swift justice. By His mercy, He faithfully acted in the best interest of His people, and through His justice, He was always faithful to His word.

Let us never forget—God desires that all of our work and our worship be motivated by genuine heartfelt devotion to Him. Because He is faithful, we know He will be merciful to us. Yet, we all know He will not tolerate rebellion against Him. His faithful and unselfish love should lead us to dedicate ourselves to Him, and we should never take His mercy for granted. Finally, like Samuel and all of the patriarchs, kings, prophets, and all of us today, we should be confident that God has blessed us. Remember this: by praising God for all of our lives, we acknowledge His ultimate control over all things in our lives.

When David knew that the hour had come for him to enter upon the work that he had been asked of God to do, of reigning over the people of Israel, He immediately recognized the true King Jehovah. He tried never to take a step of any kind without inquiring the will of that king. The fact that a man is certainly called of God to do any definite work, that man is never free from asking God to direct his every step. We are never anointed to serve and then left to find out for ourselves the way to go about our work. God is always available to those who He calls to work for Him in any way.

Yes, dear friend, that time is never wasted in which a man stops to pray or to talk to God about his desires. That time is worse than wasted when anyone tries to serve God without having first, in even the smallest detail, sought from God His personal possession. That, my friend, is wisdom in action. Let us imitate the trust and faith that David exhibited in his hour of need. He was aware that his attempt at self-sufficiency actually hindered God's work. When we pray for anything, we are to wait in a spirit of praise, and then do only what God would have us do.

We know how difficult it is to rescue a drowning man who tries to help his rescuer, and it is almost impossible for God to fight our battles when we insist upon trying to fight them ourselves. It isn't that God will not, but he cannot. Our interference hinders His working. It takes time for God to answer our prayers. I'll be the first to admit that we do not give God a chance to answer them. I live out here in farmland. God takes the earth, pulverizes it, softens it, enriches it, wets it with rain, and all these take time. We plant, till, wait, and then trust that God's way will succeed. We simply must give God a chance in His own time to work. This applies directly to our prayer life. It takes time for God to answer our prayer, and we must use our God-given wisdom to understand His time and working process.

Wisdom in action is best defined, and exemplified, by following God's directions as we place Him in control of our lives.

And speaking of wisdom, Samuel is Hebrew for "heard of God." As Moses was, Samuel was also shaped by God. Samuel was God's man at the turning point in Israel's history, and so you ask, why Samuel? God worked through Samuel because he was willing to be one thing: God's servant. Another exciting point in this choice was that Samuel "moved up the ladder," so to speak, because he was willing to listen to God's directions. Do you follow God's directions of where He wants you to go? Remember, you must turn over to God the control and the destination of your life. This, my friend, is called wisdom in action. Now you are able to be shaped as Samuel was. He was called to fill many different roles: judge, priest, prophet, and counselor. You must choose your destiny by "listening to God" and then by following His directions.

For an example, read how it worked for David. David took that corrupt kingdom left by Saul and built a strong, united power. He listened, obeyed, and followed directions. He had a heart for God. Oh, yes, we might not have David's earthly success, but following God is, by all means, the most successful and the wisest decision we can make. Keep in mind though that David realized that the Lord was behind his success because He wanted to bless Isreal. David did not become king over all of Israel until he was thirty-seven years old, even though he had been promised the kingdom many years before. Now, it was during these years that David had to wait patiently for the fulfillment of God's promise. If you feel pressured to achieve instant results and success, remember David's patience. Just as David's time of waiting prepared him for his important task, a waiting period may help to prepare you by strengthening your character and to continue to develop needed wisdom.

One sign of wisdom in our lives can be seen by the heartfelt praise that we continuously offer up to God. David praised God wholeheartedly. We can praise Him when we offer up our prayers when we recognize and thank Him for our abundant blessings and, perhaps, most especially for our enduring, loving relationship with Him. Since the Israelites first entered the Promised Land under Joshua, they had been struggling to unite the nation and drive out the wicked inhabitants. Now, after four hundred years, Israel was finally at peace. David had accomplished what no other leader before him had done. He ruled by dedicating Himself to God and to the well-being of the people.

David recognized and confessed his sins to God. He remained loyal to God throughout his lifetime. Let's pause here to meditate upon that thought for a moment. Let you and I, at this point, praise God for all of the wonderful blessings that we have received from Him and follow our praise with prayer that we too promise to follow, obey, and remain loyal to him for the rest of our lives.

As David was leaving his throne to his son Solomon, he instructed him to "serve God with wholehearted devotion...for the Lord searches every heart, and understands every motive behind the thoughts." My friend, you and I both know that nothing can be hidden from God. David was talking to his son Solomon—and to us—"Be always completely open to God, and devoted to Him." True, it makes no sense to try to hide thoughts or actions from our all-knowing, and Almighty God.

This, dear reader, should bring great joy into our lives, not fear, because God knows even the worst about us and loves us anyway. In Psalm 27:14, David said, "Wait on the

Lord, be of good courage and He shall strengthen thine heart: Wait I say on the Lord."

Now, you and I both see considerable difficulties and confusion all around us. There is an incredible increase in crimes of all types. And to make things worse for all of us, the cost of living continues to rise and is an ongoing problem. People's hearts are troubled and filled with fear. Even in David's day, there was much to cause fear. He said that it was his faith that gave him strength to look away from the world and to look to God who created the world, the goodness of God in nature, and the goodness and the faithfulness of God in His own children. This truly deepened his trust in our Heavenly Father.

Yes, dear friend, the secret of the strength and courage needed to live in our world is found in this little four-letter word—*wait*—on the Lord. As you are probably well aware, this ability is not easy to acquire. We do not like to wait in line or in the doctor's office or just to wait at all. However, waiting on the Lord is seeking His face for guidance and direction in our lives. If we do not take time to wait upon Him, we might cause a situation that we'll later regret. We must learn to remain quiet enough before we can hear His voice. Wait. His clock and His calendar are not always the same as ours, but they are always right on time.

In Psalm 63:1, David said, "O God, Thou art my God; early will I seek Thee, my flesh longeth for Thee in a dry and thirsty land, where no water is." I would say that while

David was alone in the wilderness, he was thinking of the times when God was very real to him in the Tabernacle. He still desired the reality of God's presence that he had felt in the past. He said, "O God, Thou art my God." From the very depths of his soul, he cried out, "My Soul thirsteth for Thee, my flesh longs for Thee in a dry and thirsty land, where no water is."

Dear reader, I can assure you that there are many hunger and thirsts in this world today. Some people hunger for status and power. Some hunger for pleasure, love, or even acceptance. In other words, my friend, people are searching everywhere for things that will satisfy them. Surely, you and I know that satisfaction does not come from other things. Let's look at the very words of our Lord Jesus Christ: "Blessed are they which do hunger and thirst after Righteousness; for they shall be filled." Yes, our soul's fulfillment comes only from the Lord.

David said, "Early I will seek Him." So, when we read the Bible, we must see Him in its pages. When we pray, we must be quiet enough to hear Him speak to us. We must focus our entire being upon God alone.

Dear Friend, today, are you searching for inner peace? Are you looking for something to satisfy you? You can be satisfied. You can have inner fulfillment as you seek it and find it in Jesus Christ. Christ said, "If any man thirsts, let him come to me and drink."

Tell Him today of the longing in your heart. Seek Him in God's Holy Word. Talk to Him and let Him talk to you in prayer. Today, your longing will be filled in Him!

In 1 Chronicles 29:28, David "died in a good old age, full of days, riches, and honor." These words describe the passage of King David. He had truly been a great ruler, and he was indeed a great man. Few men or women in the Bible were as close to God as David was. His daily contact with God increased his capacity to worship and praise God wholeheartedly. David's life shows us the importance of staying close to God. You and I can stay close to God through Bible study, prayer, praise and worship, along with our obedience to His Word, and by our communicating with Him on a daily basis.

Let us, in our own lives, continue as David recommended—make the Lord our greatest passion. When you and I claim to love God, we must give our relationship with Him priority over all of our possessions and over our vocation as well as over all other relationships. In our devotion to God, David said, "Delight yourself in the Lord, and He will give you the desires of your heart." This is pure heavenly wisdom.

Let us make this point clear—God wants us to enjoy pleasures. He wants His children to use all of the resources available, all that He has given us, to enjoy life. For instance, God has made it possible for me to travel all around the world. I have enjoyed immensely the wonders of His magnificent creation. However, the key to enjoying life is to delight in Him above all else. God's rightful place is as Lord of our life and to give anything else that position put us in peril.

The human heart is naturally selfish, and sometimes even destructive. Isn't it true that when God is not your top priority, you will probably give in to chasing after earthly possessions? And yet, when He is our first love, those non-productive cravings can be replaced by desires that are closer to His ways and His purpose for us.

King David, a man who faced great tragedy and heart-ache, learned from experience that a heart devoted to the Lord also experiences delight and blessings. Throughout Psalm 37, David encourages us to seek God as diligently as he had done in his life. Dear reader, will you take David's words to heart and let the Lord be your obsession? You will be amazed at how He will bless you. Take David's word for it. Obviously, he was a man that enjoyed a close, loving relationship with God, was filled with the power of the Holy Spirit, and was blessed with an abundance of His heavenly wisdom.

God warned His people about their sins. He continually restored them to His favor only to see them turn away. Eventually, the problem was beyond healing. So, where do we go from here? We must beware of allowing sin to find a dwelling place in our hearts. Yes, the day will come when there is no cure and God's judgment will replace His mercy.

Sin, often repeated but never repented of, is an invitation to disaster.

Remember, even when we choose God's way to life, we still face both blessings and troubles, joy and grief, success and failures. Throughout it all, God is there for us—guiding, encouraging, comforting, and caring.

As our wise and faithful life draws to an end, we will know that God's way is the right way. This will bring us to praise God for leading us down His path of righteousness and for assuring us of a place in His eternal kingdom. This, my dear Christian friend, is wisdom in action.

Heavenly Father, we are so often troubled in our minds, knowing so well we have full faith in you, and yet our conscience continues to accuse us. We know, Father, that there is nothing we can offer that can attract the love of one who is Holy, and as loving as you are. Yet, you have declared your unchanging love for us in your Son, Jesus Christ. We know that if nothing in us can win your love, nothing can stop you from loving us. Yes, Lord, your love is un-caused, and very much undeserved. Help us to believe the intensity, the eternity of the love that you do have for us. May your love cast out all of our fear; may our troubled hearts and minds be at peace. May we trust not in what we are, but always in what you have declared Thyself to be. Amen.

Solomon

There is a beautiful event in the early years of King Solomon's reign as he succeeded his father David. Just after he went up to the throne, the Lord appeared to him and gave him the right to choose any blessing he desired. Instead of choosing wealth, power, a long life, he simply asked for wisdom. God was so pleased with him for this simple single choice that He gave him not only wisdom, but all of the other blessings as well.

Solomon gained fame for his superhuman wisdom, and many of his sayings can be found throughout the book of Proverbs—"Solomon's Pearls of Wisdom."

> "Wisdom calls aloud in the street; she raises her voice in the public street."
>
> "At the head of the noisy street, she cries out! In the gateway of the city she cries out."
>
> "How long will you simple ones love your simple ways? How long will mockers delight in mockery, and fools hate knowledge?"

> "If you had responded to my rebuke, I would have poured out my heart to you, and made my thoughts known to you."

King Solomon not only built the temple, but he also gave us the teachings and doings of the Holy Spirit in our everyday lives. The key word that signifies everything in King Solomon's life and works is *wisdom*. Wisdom can be obtained through God, the person of Jesus Christ, and the Holy Spirit.

All of the wisdom of the ages has come from those sources, from their eternal minds. Not only do they represent the wisdom and the power of God, but they also represent a love that is for us, and it will be for us right into eternity. It is His wisdom that has inspired every high and mighty thought of man. This wisdom has inspired every touch of human genius. God is the foundation of all life, truth, power, and wisdom. He wants to be our wisdom, our guide, our power, and our complete earthly existence.

Surely, my dear friend, we must listen to His gentle voice as He calls us into a close personal relationship with Him. His words say it all: "Now, therefore, hearken unto me, ye children, for Blessed are they that kept my ways. Hear instruction, and be wise, and refuse it not; for who finds me finds life, and shall obtain the favor of the Lord, but he that sins against me wrongs his own Soul, and they that hate me, loves Death." So, look at it this way: there are two houses standing face-to-face on the highway of life. You have the heavenly house, with the Holy Ghost standing at the front door and inviting the children of sin and sorrow and saying to them, "Come, everyone that is thirsty, come have bread and milk, without money at all. Why waste your money for things that are not bread and milk?"

And right across the road, people from everywhere are running by, charging into the house of pleasure, the house of shame, the house of sin, and dashing straight into the gates of hell.

That pretty much well explains it for us. Wisdom is listening to the Holy Spirit, the house of heavenly righteousness, which is calling us to His glory, His power, His mercy, His peace, His love, and His grace. Let's face it—most of us are poor listeners. Are you aware of your listening bias? Many of us tend to tune out children or old people. For years, many women have complained that men do not listen to them as carefully as they listen to other men. When we are angry about something, do we carefully listen to an explanation?

True, the world cries out for good listeners. Doctors will tell you that they see patients on a daily basis who have nothing physically wrong with them. They merely need someone to listen to them. As a retired high school teacher, I can guarantee you that over the many years of teaching and talking to thousands of students, I watched the good listeners become successful in their life's endeavors. Good listeners in the world today are so rare that they are in heavy demand.

Along that same line, when life caves in, you do not need someone telling you of the reasons. Wisdom tells you that what they need is comfort. They are not interested in answers; they need some one. Thankfully, Jesus, through the Holy Spirit, does not come with an explanation; He comes to us with His presence. God does not reveal His plan; He reveals Himself. He comes to us in warm and loving fellowship when we are cold and alone. He gives us His peace when we are troubled, His strength when we are weak, His courage when we are afraid, His songs when we are sad, and His bread when we are hungry.

Yes, dear reader, He is with us on our journeys. He is there when we are at home. He sits with us at our dinner table. He knows about funerals, weddings, commencements, hospitals, jails, unemployment, laughter, rest, and tears. He knows because He is with us. He comes to us again and again, wherever and whenever we call.

I am asking you, my dear Christian friend, to think about how meaningless life would be without Him. Yes, to ponder on the fact that our lives are regulated and controlled by His loving hand and how wonderfully we are blessed by His soul-soothing presence. Are you listening for His precious Word? Ah, yes, you have activated His heavenly wisdom!

There is much to be said for the person who learns to listen instead of talk. When we listen, we learn, and when we talk, we block learning. A fool loves to hear the sound of his own voice, but the wise person rejoices in what can be heard. We need to learn to listen so that we can honestly help the people who come to us for guidance. When we insist upon doing the talking, we are being foolish, and we present an example that we cannot be proud of. God wants us to deal with people through love, and most people need to feel that they are being heard. Wisdom—the reward that we get from a lifetime of listening when we'd rather talk.

Heavenly Father, I know that you listen to me. Teach me to listen, that I might be a blessing to those in need. I want to learn all I can, and it is in silence that understanding comes. Amen.

Never allow your ego to replace God's wisdom. God wants us to humble ourselves, and to except His mercy and grace.

This, my friend, is the message of wisdom—seek and search for its treasure and be blessed, for "happy is the man that finds wisdom, and he who gets understanding...her ways are pleasantness, and all her paths are peace. She is a tree of life to them that lay hold upon her, and happy is everyone that possesses her."

I was approximately twelve years old when I had a neighbor boy who wanted me to be his friend. He came to our house a few times, but my dad discouraged it. He told me that he didn't think the boy's attitude was right for me and thought that I could get into trouble with him. I simply could not understand what he meant at all. However, I did take his word for it and eased out of the friendship as delicately as possible. I did not make the boy feel bad about it, and I guess you are wondering how it all turned out. Well, sorry to say, but just a year or so later, the boy was caught in a burglary, and a year or so after that, he was caught stealing an automobile. I felt so sorry for the boy, but I sure thanked my dad.

From this seemingly insignificant little event, I learned a very significant lesson. When a person thinks they have all of the answers, and they refuse to listen to others, there can be trouble. You might think that if I had talked to the boy over a period of time, he might have changed. And yet, wisdom could say to you, "If you jump into a puddle of mud, will the mud come out cleaner, or would you, perhaps, come out muddier?" I am convinced that it is the wise person that seeks counsel from those that they trust and in those whom they have faith with. Without effective counseling, things can go seriously wrong. And yet, when good and effective counselors are available, and their advice is followed, plans can proceed smoothly. The best counsel we can seek is the Lord's. He will guide us if we ask Him. When we shut the Lord out of our decisions, we are destined for failure. Obedience to the Lord is wisdom in action.

Lesson learned: God is more than willing to pour out His heart and make His thoughts known to us. To receive His advice, we must be willing to listen, refusing to let ego stand in our way. Ego is thinking more highly of our own wisdom and desires than of God's. If we think we know better than God or feel we have no need of God's counsel, we have fallen into foolish and disastrous pride.

Write this on the tablet of your heart: God wants us to recognize our helplessness so that we do not lapse into a false sense of security. God wants us to humble ourselves and to find comfort in His mercy and grace. As far as humans are concerned, no one is better or holier than the next person. Thankfully, through the wisdom of the Holy Spirit, God does protect us from delving too seriously into sin. But if we were to withdraw His hand, we might be drawn into deadly depths. And so, my friend, God does teach us to humble ourselves in His presence and to continually pray for guidance through the Holy Spirit.

In Psalms, we read: "The Lord foils the plans of nations." When so-called wise men ignore God's Word, He doesn't let any of their plans succeed, whether good or bad. God will always block the plans of those who work the hardest by using their own wisdom. Our plans will cause us serious problems, and they will trouble us. God does not want this trouble to destroy us; He is simply trying to get us to give up our foolish ideas and plans. He really wants to show us that our wisdom is worthless.

Solomon recognized the fact that wisdom is a gift from God. We must look to God for His wisdom. What are the Seven Pillars of Wisdom?

In the final analysis, our wisdom is not what makes our plans a success. Only God's wisdom, as we receive it from the Holy Spirit, can satisfy our every need, so we must learn to pray, "Let your will be done!"

A good quote for us today: "Common sense suits itself to the ways of the world. Wisdom tries to conform to the ways of Heaven." We have a rather strange story coming from the reign of King Solomon—two women, making a claim for the same baby, go to King Solomon for judgment. The first woman says, "Three days after I gave birth, this woman, who lives in the same house, had her child. Her baby died and in the middle of the night she got up and switched babies with me." The second woman denies the story, saying that the living baby is hers. It was quite a dilemma for King Solomon, and even stranger yet is the king's solution: cut the baby in half and give half a child to each mother.

The real mother, of course, cannot bear to see her infant son die, so she pleads, "Give the living baby to her! Do not let him die!" Solomon, realizing that no true mother would sacrifice her baby's life to prove a point, said, "Give the living baby to the first woman. Do not kill him; she is his mother." When all Israel heard the verdict given, they held King Solomon in awe because they saw that he had wisdom from God to administer justice.

Yes, dear friend, Solomon obviously realized something that we often forget: knowledge is gotten through study, power can be gained through force, and honor can be acquired by deeds of greatness. But wisdom is a gift from God. The key to Solomon's wisdom was simply the fact that he realized he needed it. Many times we depend upon ourselves, our instincts, training, education, and even our reputation, rather than looking to God for His wisdom. However, being wise doesn't mean knowing everything, memorizing scriptures, or having your name on degrees. It does mean being able to see situations from God's point of view.

Let's put it this way: depending upon the Almighty God is ultimate wisdom. In other words, let no one think that wisdom can be obtained by worldly means, and definitely not by accident. You must turn from the sinful ways, humble yourself, admit your need, confess what you are lacking, and ask God for help.

Wisdom takes time, moments of quiet reflection, and definitely keeping an ear open to God in prayer plus delving into Bible study on a regular basis. Wisdom will not come overnight, but it will come over time.

A question for you: What are the Seven Pillars of WISDOM as found in the Bible?

1. Prudence - doing the right thing.
2. Knowledge - doing what is truly right as acquired rightly.
3. Discretion - actions based on truth
4. Counsel - dispensing truth
5. Sound Judgment - decision making, right from wrong
6. Understanding - applied knowledge
7. Power - ability to get right things done

Prayer

Help me not to trust so much in my own wisdom, Heavenly Father. Let me see that there are many things that I have yet to learn. Give me patience and perseverance that I might come to know that which will save me from my own foolishness. Amen.

Isaiah

The book of Isaiah is the first of the writings of the prophets in the Bible, and Isaiah, the author, is generally considered to be one of the greatest prophets ever.

I personally feel that by bringing the wisdom of this great prophet to your attention, you will gain a deeper understanding of the messages of this strong and courageous man of God and of his fearless proclaiming of God's Holy Word.

Dear reader, I pray that you will listen to his words of wisdom, that you will accept them in relation to your own life, and that his wisdom will lead you to return, repent, and to be renewed. May these uplifting messages lead you to trust in God's redemption through Jesus Christ. Rejoice, your Savior has come, and He is coming again. Amen.

It has been said that trees and prophets are both planted for the future, and yet, many times the results are either forgotten or overlooked. It is especially true in the life of Isaiah. The people of his day could have been rescued by his messages from God, but they refused to listen. Sounds familiar? Isaiah did not start out to be a prophet. At the time of King Uzziah's death, Isaiah was a scribe in the royal palace of Jerusalem. God had other plans for Isaiah, and his call from God left no doubt what moved him to become a prophet. The call permanently affected the heart, the character, and the life of Isaiah. His call has the same effect on us today. Isaiah's testimony is that his message came from the one and only one—God Himself. God told Isaiah that the people would not listen, but that he should deliver the message anyway, since He knew that eventually many would listen. In Isaiah 6:13, God said, "And though a tenth remains in the Land, it will again be laid waste. But as the terebinth and the oak leave stumps when they are cut down, so the Holy seed will be the stump in the Land."

Dear reader, you and I are a part of that "stump," that future that has seen many of God's promises fulfilled in Jesus Christ. We too have attained the hope that God is still active in the history of His creation in our own world today. Accept the most precious lesson from the message of Isaiah and learn that God's help is needed in order to be able to face the sins of those whom we are counseling. We all know that we must accept God's forgiveness and that we are to share that forgiveness with all people. Show others that God is purely and perfectly holy, just, and merciful in His almighty love.

In the year that King Uzziah died, Isaiah received his commission to be God's messenger to His people. Isaiah 6:1–8 says:

> In the year that King Uzziah died, I saw the Lord, seated on a throne, high and exalted, and the train of His robe filled the Temple. About him were Seraphs, each with six wings: With two wings they covered their faces, with two they covered their feet, and with two they were flying: And they were calling to one another: "Holy, holy, holy is the Lord Almighty; the whole earth is full of His Glory." At the sound of their voices the doorposts and the thresholds shook, and the Temple was filled with smoke. "Woe to me!" I cried. "I am ruined! For I am a man of unclean lips, and I live among a people of unclean lips, and my eyes have seen the King, the Lord Almighty." Then one of the Seraphs flew to me with a live coal in his hand, which he had taken with tongs from the Altar, with it he touched my mouth and said, "See, this has touched you lips; your guilt is taken away and your sin is atoned for." Then I heard the voice of the Lord saying, "Whom shall I send? And whom shall go for us?" And I said, "Hear am I. Send me."

My dear Christian friend, look at it this way: Uzziah had been king longer than any other person in all of Jewish history. He was the only king whom Isaiah ever knew. I believe that Uzziah's death probably broke him to a point of disbelief. And then, to face God with the brilliance of His presence must have shaken him right out of his sandals. However, he was stunned in seeing the totally unshakeable God standing there before him. What would that do to you if it were you?

Back in those days, men of strong faith were said to "walk in fear of God." Whenever God appeared to men in those days, they had an overwhelming sense of terror and dread, a sense of sinfulness and guilt. When God spoke, Abraham stretched himself out on the ground to listen. When Moses saw the Lord in the burning bush, he hid his face in fear of God. Isaiah cried, "Woe is me! I am undone because I am a man of unclean lips." I would suppose that from all of these accounts, if we were to see the transforming presence of God face-to-face, the fight would leave us instantly, and we would very meekly ask, "Lord, what will you have me do?" His wisdom would lead us to his will.

One of the first messages that God had for Isaiah had to do with the fact that He loathed and was filled to the limit with their lack of true moral and spiritual expression in their worship services. He was calling for a new attitude in all of their religious observances. The singing of hymns, their offering of prayers, the giving of money, the study of His Holy Word all became hateful to God. God desires for the spiritual and moral condition of the worshipers to be more in line, more suited to what these things stand for. He was calling for more sincere faith and devotion. These worship services were meant to be an outward sign of their inward faith of God, but they had become empty due to the lack of inward faith. I might venture to say that many worship services today have come to place more faith in the ritual itself than in the God they worship.

Wisdom would ask you and me to examine our own worship experiences. Is it just entertainment as you enjoy that wonderful music and just going along with what others are doing? Or is it genuine, heartfelt praise to our Father God? God takes His pleasure from seeing us with our inward faith, exalting Him. God wants us to love Him, trust Him, turn from our sins, and then He will be pleased with our several services of worship, whether it be with time, money, or in the fellowship of praise.

To those who live in close fellowship with God, His wisdom is victorious. Let God purify you. Make His wisdom the dominant factor in your life.

You and I and all other Christians should rejoice in the fact that in spite of the darkness and the degenerative attitudes of worship, Isaiah had a clear vision of the final result, of the ultimate glory, and the unwavering faith that would one day be realized. Surely, you know that all the prophetic writings have clearly shown that one day we shall "walk in the light," that righteousness will triumph, and we shall walk in the hope and the glory of Almighty God.

Let us pause to meditate upon that for a while. In the days of darkness and widespread corruption, we are apt to forget, or even to doubt, the ultimate triumph of God. This never happens to those who live in close fellowship with God. His wisdom is victorious. We have learned that when Uzziah died, a period of darkness descended on Israel, and in the period of sadness and mourning, Isaiah was given a vision of God, high and lifted up.

Let me ask you, was this a coincidence? Personally, I don't think it was. I believe that in God's own way, Uzziah's death caused in Isaiah a spiritual dilemma that made him ready to lift his focus from earth to heaven, and I believe that this happens to us even today. We look up only when tragedy strikes us, devastates us, and puts us flat on our backs. Our earthly thoughts must be removed before we can see the glory of our Heavenly Father, Almighty God. Wisdom leads us to see that our trust must always be in God. Otherwise, He will bring us down to a condition in which we will be completely dependent upon Him. Oh, yes, letting God purify us may be painful, but we must be purified before we can truly represent God, who is pure and holy.

I must ask, am I talking to someone right now who lately has been knocked for a loop? Things that you have depended upon are no longer there? Then listen to me: God is not angry with you. He simply wants you to rest your weight fully upon Him. Our earthly focus must be removed before we can see the glory of God. The sooner we learn to make God our foundation, the better we are going to be able to face some dark and difficult days ahead. We are seeing in these very days that our great nation, the United States of America, is being shaken so that we may return to the unshakeable kingdom of the Almighty God.

We may yet say, "In the year that all of my hopes and dreams came crashing down, I saw the Lord!" The grace of God does not come to put the soul of man at rest until he returns and surrenders fully to Him. In Job 42:5–6, we read him saying, "My ears have heard of you, but now my eyes have seen you. Therefore, I despise myself and repent in dust and ashes." Wisdom had arrived.

Christ Is My Master

The longer I am alive, the harder I strive,
    Draw nearer to God and His blessings,
Knowing after all, even a sparrow cannot fall
    From His grace and His gentle caressing.

As I go through this life, with its toil and its strife,
    I've had sorrows that I'd rather forget,
But I struggle along with a smile and a song,
    Always remembering—"I am not home yet!"

> When Satan comes crawling
> > On his belly and calling,
> Tempting me to step into disaster,
> > I look into the eyes of the father of lies
> And tell him that Christ is my Master!

—Russell Young

When will we listen to His still small voice? Must we go through calamities before we will listen to God's words? Think and consider what God may be telling you and obey Him before time runs out. Knowing what God wants you to do and then doing it shows the wisdom in His Word.

Isaiah's next prophetic words brought joy to the people of Israel, and it is still bringing joy to the world today. This message that God gave to the world is doubly exciting to me because, believe it or not, I am writing these prophetic words just ten days before Christmas. Isaiah brought the message from God to tell the people of the coming destruction of the enemies of the nation, and much more fantastic than that news, he informed the faithful souls around him of the coming of the Messianic kingdom. He told them of the character of the Messiah, of His method of rule, a glowing description of His reign, and he told them how the scattered people would be gathered from the four corners of the earth. These words were far and away the most magnificent and the most heart-rending words ever spoken about the kingdom of heaven, which was yet to be.

He explained how the kingdom of God was based upon the wisdom of God, resulting in perfect understanding. He said that Christ came as the anointed and appointed king, Himself being human, a child born to us, a Son given. This brings great joy to the people because the one who is great in their midst is holy. He explained that the coming departure from evil will ensure the victory. The city and the kingdom will be stable and permanent, having no end, and this leads to the supreme joy of celebrating His reign and our salvation.

Isaiah 9:2 says, "The people walking in darkness have seen a great light; on those living in the shadow of death a light has dawned." Verse 6 says, "For unto us a child is born, to us a Son is given, and the government shall be on His shoulders. And He will be called wonderful counselor, mighty God, everlasting Father, prince of peace."

All for You

When God sent His Son to earth,
  By Mary's sacred virgin birth,
And proved to man His love's worth,
  He did it all for you.

When His touch made the blind see,
  Healed the sick, made the captive free,
Raised the dead, and calmed the sea,
  He did it all for you.

131

When He was taken on that dark night,
    He never argued, showed no fright,
Solemnly revealed His spiritual might,
    He did it all for you.

When He was shamefully led to Calvary,
    Scourged by a mob on a violent spree,
Crowned with thorns and nailed to a tree,
    He did it all for you.

When the empty tomb was opened wide,
    And redemptive work fully satisfied,
And returned to live at the Father's side,
    He did it all for you.

When you joyfully arrive at Heaven's place,
    Where love abounds in blissful grace,
Being held in the Savior's sweet embrace,
    You will know it is true—
Yes! He did it all for you.

—Russell Young

Let us, all of us brothers and sisters in Christ, be glad and rejoice today because "He has come!" and may our hearts go out to those people, wherever and whomever they may be, who have no blessed Christmas day. Let us never forget that the angel announced, "Behold, I bring you good tidings of great joy, which shall be to all people."

As a former high school guidance counselor, I cannot help but ponder the wonderful name given to our Lord Jesus—Wonderful Counselor! In our Guidance studies at St. Francis University in Fort Wayne, Indiana, we studied the primary techniques used to release the repressive feelings of many of our students. In the fifth Beatitude, Jesus used the word *pure*: "Blessed are the pure in heart, for they shall see God." When researching the word *pure*, I found that this word is derived from the Greek word *catharsis*, which means "to cleanse" or "make pure." Psychologists use the word *catharsis* to describe the feeling of release and cleansing that comes to a person when in the presence of a trusted friend or counselor. Under the right conditions and the right circumstances, one often feels renewed and released.

I have witnessed this reaction on several occasions after a counseling session with a student. They come with deep hurts and frustrations, and when they are sure they are in the presence of someone they can trust, they open up their repressed feelings in such a way that they express it beautifully—"I feel so different. It is like someone has reached down inside me and scraped my insides clean." I ask you, what gives them this feeling of joyful release? It comes only in the presence of mutual confidence and trust. When a counselor shows disapproval or shock, there is no release (catharsis) realized. Psychologists will tell you that this only happens when a counselor is warm and accepting and never when harsh or judgmental.

Now, my dear friend, it becomes absolutely obvious that when in the presence of Jesus, the Wonderful Counselor, we have the possibility of experiencing the deepest catharsis, purity of heart, that it is possible to obtain. Yes, the word is *wisdom*!

Prayer

Blessed Jesus, my Counselor, my friend, help me to open up my entire being to you that I might receive complete catharsis. I do not want just to be clean, but to be wholly cleansed in your name's sake. Amen.

"Blessed are those who hunger and thirst for Righteousness." We are thirsting for the One who can make us right again.

Isaiah, God's messenger, sends these words to us directly from God: "Thus sayeth Jehovah: Keep ye justice, and do righteous; for my salvation is near to come, and my righteousness to be revealed." These are the words of God sent to us in regard to the salvation and the righteousness that came to us through the appearing of His Son, the servant of God. They were always near in God's purpose, but due to the persistent failure of His people, centuries passed before He came.

But He did come, and He did fulfill His promise. Of course, it will be completed when He comes again, without sin, for our salvation. Yes, it is postponed. Why? Because His message is still being refused by those who are disloyal and those who are refusing to accept His precious words. It remains for you and me and all who love His name and wait for His coming to keep justice and to do righteousness. When He does return, there will be no escape from Him. All evil and nonbelievers alike will be overcome, cast out, and destroyed. Does this sound too harsh? Well, keep in mind that God's wrath is thrown against those ones who brought on the desolation and destruction of men. It is His fierceness against all that destroys love, and justice, and righteousness.

Another message from God through Isaiah is: "Are you not to share your food with the hungry, and to provide the poor wanderer with shelter—when you see the naked, to clothe them, and not to turn away from your own flesh and blood?" Then, your light will shine like the dawn, and your healing will quickly appear, your righteousness will go before you, and the glory of the Lord will protect you. Then, you will call, and the Lord will answer. You will cry for help, and He will say, "Here am I."

Dear reader, please remember: we are not only commanded to seek the kingdom of God, but His righteousness as well. I know that to a lot of Christians, righteousness is seen as tithing or faithful church attendance or loving others. Well, these are Christian responsibilities, but they are only the beginning of holy living. Righteousness was well defined by God at Mt. Sinai and by the prophets, and finally by the life of His Son, Lord Jesus. God's definition of righteousness is based upon justice for all people, especially for the unfortunate, care for the widows and orphans, hating evil, and doing good.

When it comes to defining righteousness, I think immediately of John 7:37 where Jesus said, "If anyone is thirsty, let him come to me and drink." Now, I know most of us are not apt to admit our thirsts. We try to cover them up with false cravings and with desires that have not satisfied the true thirsts, and they never will. Eventually, our world caves in on us, and we are left with the reality of a parched and dying existence. "God, I need help!"

Sure, we are thirsty—very thirsty—but we cover it up by thirsting for fame or stuff, or even romance. Yes, we have sipped from those wells, but they will never quench our thirsts; they kill. "Blessed are those who hunger and thirst for righteousness!"

Yes, righteousness—that is it. That is what we are thirsty for. We are thirsty for a clean conscience. In fact, we thirst for a fresh start. We are thirsting for the "one" who can make us right again. And let us look at what God, through Isaiah, has to say about this "one" for whom we are waiting and living in expectation. God speaks in Isaiah 42:1–4, "Behold my servant, whom I uphold, my chosen one, in whom my soul delights; I have put my Spirit upon him so that he might pronounce judgment on the nations. He will not cry or lift up His voice or make it heard in the street; a bent reed He will not break, and a dimly burning wick He will not quench; He will pronounce judgment according to the truth. He will not fail or be discouraged till He has administered judgment on the earth; and the coast lands wait for His Law!"

Dear reader, God, speaking through the prophet Isaiah, is proclaiming that the one chosen to appear was equipped with the Holy Spirit. He was not a self-appointed savior of humanity. God's damaged creation could only be put right by His servant—selected, chosen, and empowered to do so by God Himself. Yes, Christ was the anointed one (not appointed by Himself). He accepted the task from the Lord of Hosts, His Father. It is written: "My servant, my chosen one, in whom my soul delights." Yes, the task of the anointed brings judgment to all nations. He leads us to a correct relationship with God, with our neighbors, and with all the earth.

Again, Isaiah prophesied, "He shall not judge by what His ears hear, but with righteousness, He shall judge the poor and decide for the meek of the earth. All of this, including the lamb that lies down beside the wolf—is what God's judgment will bring about. No one shall do harm or evil any longer." This is the task that God's servant was given—to remove sin, correct injustice, end wars, destroy pride, and help the weak and the powerless. How will He do all of this? Not as we probably would—by raising our voices, preaching loudly to those in the streets, not by government or enforcement agents. That is not the way of our Lord Jesus Christ. He went about preaching, healing the sick, and forgiving sins quietly and inconspicuously. Jesus was gentle and humble of heart. He chose to use this method. Think about it—how did Jesus call you and attract you? How did He gain your trust and faith? Was it by shouting at you, or was it through His quietness and His love? He came among sinners, and it was here that the work of atonement began. He didn't crush us. He came to us, turned to us with His precious love, and invited us to join Him in this life and use His way to be put on His path of righteousness.

Yes, dear friend, this is what our Lord, God's servant, is like. He is the one we wait for and look forward to with heads held up high. He will set right our sin-filled lives and will not fail until He has placed judgment on the earth.

In righteousness, we will be blessed to overflowing with His Wisdom.

Isaiah, the prophet, has another message from God for us. "But now, this is what the Lord says—He who created you, O Jacob, He who formed you O Israel: 'Fear not, for I have redeemed you; I have called you by name; you are mine. When you pass through the waters, I will be with you; And when you pass through the rivers, they will not sweep over you. When you walk through the fire, you will not be burned; the flames will not set you ablaze. For I am the Lord, your God, the Holy One of Israel, your Savior.'"

Yes, we are redeemed. We've been called by name, and, along with His judgment, His holy righteousness is within reach. Praise His holy name!

And now, dear reader, let us travel together down that road to righteousness. Think of it as a one-way, four-lane highway leading us to that magnificent state of holy righteousness. As we travel along, we will need to stop for rest at the Seven Pillars of Wisdom.

> Prudence—caution, deliberation, foresight
> Knowledge—learning, enlightenment, insight
> Deliberation—determine, discover, discriminate
> Counsel—guidance, instruction, advice
> Sound Judgment—rationality, acuteness, awareness
> Understanding—intelligence, perception, thought
> Power—strength, vigor, stamina

When we reach that great state of righteousness, we will be in a true and eternal loving relationship with the Lord. We will be blessed to overflowing with His wisdom, and He will anoint us as servants of Man. Yes, His Son, the Servant of God, has chosen us to complete the work that He began some two thousand years ago. Our wisdom is to be put into action.

Yes, dear friend, it is true that many times the most difficult evils to overcome are in your secret souls, unseen and unknown by anyone but Jesus. They are harder than any open battles on your face. In those victories, the crown is to be won. May God help you overcome and be victorious over evil that you may wear the crown.

> O Father, self-sufficient as Thou art,
> Come to bless my aching heart,
> Hold me in Thy precious love,
> O Lord, from Thy gracious power mercy flows
> Into my life, and heaven knows
> I yearn to be with thee above.
> Amen.

—Russell Young

Be richly blessed and attain His righteousness through His wisdom.

Isaiah closes his prophesies in 66:22–24: "'As the new Heavens and the new earth that I make will endure for me,' declares the Lord, 'So will your name and descendants endure. From one new moon to another, and from one Sabbath to another, all mankind will come and bow down before me,' says the Lord. 'And they will go out and look for the dead bodies of those who rebelled against me; their worm will not die, nor will their fire be quenched, and they will be loathsome to all mankind.'"

As we can see, for the faithless ones, there is a dreadful judgment given. And for those who are faithful, there is a glorious reward. "Your name and your descendants will endure." Doesn't this make you want to believe that everyone would want to followthe Lord? But we are just as rebellious, foolish, and reluctant to change as Israel was. We are often just as negligent in feeding the hungry, working for justice, obeying God's Word, and living for His righteousness. Make sure you are one of those who will be richly blessed and one who obtains His righteousness through His wisdom. James 3: 13 says, "Who is wise and understanding among you? Let him show it by his good life, by deeds done in the humility that comes from wisdom."

Amen.

Jeremiah

Jeremiah was a prophet in the kingdom of Judah when Jerusalem was being destroyed. God's people were being carried away to Babylon because of their sins. It was an extremely difficult time of judgment and of severe suffering for all of the people, and definitely for Jeremiah personally. But through his prophecy, we are told again and again of God's promise of their being restored after seventy years, and he constantly assured them, through Jeremiah, of the New Covenant. Yes, it is true, sin does have its consequences, and it is also true that through Christ Jesus, the Mediator, God's last word is of forgiveness and eternal life.

The word of the Lord came to me saying, "Before I formed you in the womb I knew you, before you were born I set you apart; I appointed you as a prophet to the Nations" (Jeremiah 1: 4–5), and in verses 7 to 8, "Do not say, 'I am only a child,' you must go to everyone I send you to and say whatever I command you. Do not be afraid of them, for I am with you and I will rescue you,' declares the Lord." Now, let us take a look at the conditions under which Jeremiah lived. He ministered for forty years during the captivity of the people of Judah in Babylon. In that time, he saw the rise and fall of five kings. I will say that, perhaps, Jeremiah was not the greatest prophet, but he was certainly the most courageous. Except for one brief period (under the rule of King Josiah), Jeremiah ministered for forty years in a country in which the whole trend was away from God. Everybody and everything seemed to be going downstream. There was political corruption and religious hypocrisy (sounds familiar?), and the sad part of it all was that the people going downhill were God's people!

Think of this: Jeremiah saw in his time a complete shift in world power. The power of Egypt gave way to Babylon, and to me it seems that the most shattering and difficult part of those times to comprehend was the downward trend of morality. To me, the greatest tragedy of all was that God's people were swept up in the tide of debauchery.

Dear reader, let us remember that they were God's chosen people. They were His by His Holy choice. They were His because He brought them out of Egypt and through the wilderness into a precious land in which there would flow milk and honey. They were His because they received and proved His promises.

You see, dear friend, what I am trying to show you is that they were the instruments through which He was going to fulfill His plan for a world overflowing with His love, His righteousness, His redemption, and eternal life in His glory. And yet, Jeremiah 2:13 says from God's own heart, "My people have committed two sins: They have forsaken me, the Spring of Living Water, and they have dug their own cisterns, broken cisterns that cannot hold water." Jeremiah ministers through his constant companionship with God. He is delivering this message to the people of Judah as a result of his intimate conversations with God Himself. Yes, the nation had been charged with having committed two evils. First, they had forsaken God, the "fountain of living waters." We are familiar with the "living waters" in John 7:38. They are waters rising from springs, always fresh, always flowing.

And what are cisterns? They are tanks for holding water, storing it. It has ceased to be "living"; it is stagnant and deteriorating. Hence, when these people left the "living water," they separated themselves from God. They were thirsty, so they dug wells, cisterns, and got stagnant waters. The fresh "living water" was lost to them because of their sinful ways. Cisterns break, and they will never hold water. This is precisely the way with us. We must live with the "living water" or die. The spiritual significance of Jeremiah's message is obvious to you and to me. Remain in Him and live!

Dear friend, I am convinced that we live in a day just like that of Jeremiah. Our thirsts have shifted from the moral to the immoral, from the spiritual to the non-spiritual—the earthly desires of the evil one. And I am sorry to say that we too are digging cisterns of stagnant water, unhealthy water that will only lead to our destruction. Why is this?

I am old enough to remember when there was a Bible in every home, and it was well used. There was a genuine worship of God, a distinct belief in the reading of the scriptures, and a strong, heartfelt religious conviction all around us. But our great nation is definitely fumbling the ball, letting it slip through our fingers as the Word of God is being ignored. When people develop a looseness in their morality, the nation itself becomes soft at its very root and begins to die away. The saddest part is the fact that God looks upon us, the church, and He has to say exactly what He said to Jeremiah: "My chosen people, my choice, my redemption, my purchase because I went to the Cross for them, have committed the evils!"

Dear reader and Christian friend, those words of God sting my soul. Let's face the facts: there is a war going on, and it is an eternal war. There will be no armistice until the King shall come, and we shall meet Him face-to-face. It just seems to me that the church of Jesus Christ today has lost the power. "Ye shall receive power when the Holy Ghost is come upon you." And that is the source of living water that is lacking in our lives today.

What do you suppose is God's purpose for us today? What is God looking for us to do in this great nation today?

Wisdom—God's Holy Word, as always, supplies the answer. God's purpose for us today is to produce men and women who will share the burden with the Lord, who will go to the Lord in prayer and in crying to God for revival, in leading this great nation away from the stagnant waters of greed, fortune, fame, idolatry, sexual immorality, sins, and corruptions of all kinds. Yes, to lead His people back to the source of His living waters, to Jesus Christ—the way, the truth, and the life. God's purpose is to find those who will say to God, "I won't let you go until you bless me," who will be on their faces pleading with God for revival throughout this land of ours.

Dear reader, God's purpose is to find those who will share the load with the Lord Jesus and feel the throb of His heart, share His tears, and share in His groans and agony. Pray for this stagnant nation to return to repentance and for the redemption of the living Savior, to walk in His path of righteousness, to return to a close personal relationship with Him, and to accept the power of the Holy Spirit as it comes upon you through the wisdom of His precious Word.

Yes, as I mentioned earlier, Jeremiah might not have been the greatest prophet ever, but he was the most heroic and courageous. There were days when Jeremiah would have given anything to be someone else because God's call was costing him everything. This includes his friends, his reputation, perhaps, even his life if some people were to have their way. But the fire he feared the most was the one that he had inside of him.

Join me in looking at it from another angle. Jeremiah's main complaint was with the religious and political establishment of his day—that is, the ministers and political leaders who had the responsibility of serving God's people and of leading them in righteous living. In their greed and their grasp for power—and in the grip of their bondage to sin—they had lost the credibility and wisdom to lead as God desired. I ask you, does this ring a bell? Does this remind you of what is happening in our midst today? Jeremiah would say of them, "They dress the wounds of my people as though their deficiencies are not serious." And still to this very day, when immorality and pride try to appear as authoritative leadership, the wounds go untreated. Sin escalates. Immorality increases at a disgusting rate.

Read with me these words from the very heart of Jeremiah 20: 7–12:

> O Lord, you deceived me, and I was deceived; you overpowered me and prevailed. I am ridiculed all day long; everyone mocks me. Whenever I speak, I cry out proclaiming violence and destruction. So the word of the Lord has brought me insult and reproach all day long. But if I say, "I will not mention Him, or speak anymore in His name," His word is in my heart like a fire, a fire shut up in my bones. I am weary of holding it in; indeed I cannot. I hear many whispering, "Terror on every side! Report him! Let's report him!" All my friends are waiting for me to slip, saying, "Perhaps he will be deceived;

then we will prevail over him, and take revenge on him." But the Lord is with me like a mighty warrior, so my prosecutors will stumble and not prevail. They will fail and be thoroughly disgraced; their dishonor will never be forgotten. O Lord Almighty, you who examine the righteous, and probe the heart and mind, let me see your vengeance upon them, for to you I have committed my cause.

And thus, dear friend, I ask you, how could anyone read these words from Jeremiah and not be sympathetically affected deep down in the heart and soul? However, this is where our theme—wisdom—comes into spiritual existence.

When we focus on one who is lost in sin, whether they accept Christ, thank us, praise us, agree with us or not, regardless of the final result, we are sticking our necks out and are vulnerable to pain and disappointment. We have our peace through our strong and devoted relationship with our Lord Jesus Christ. It is from Him that we receive our satisfaction. He provides His love, and that is sufficient. We are to thrive on God's gift to us—the presence and the power of the Holy Spirit. Whatever we cannot do, He can and He will do. Nothing can erase the peace of God in me when He is in control of me.

As I have said so many times, develop a close personal and loving relationship with the Lord. It will lead to peaceful contentment in your life, and through your peace, those around you will experience His peace as well. Write this on the tablet of your heart: "God gives wisdom to the faithful, and on top of that—joy!" How can you say, "We are wise, for we have the Law of the Lord" (Jeremiah 8:8–9) when actually the lying pen of the scribes has handled it falsely? The wise will be put to shame; they will be dismayed and trapped. Since they have rejected the Word of the Lord, what kind of wisdom do they have?

As we all know, men had received the Law of God. The scribe's job was to interpret the Law and apply it to the people. But they had rejected the very Word of God that they were supposed to be teaching. They were deceitfully manipulating the Laws to suit themselves, to meet their needs for fame and fortune, and, thus, changing God's message. By corrupting God's Holy Word at its very source, they were committing the most horrendous sin of all. "What kind of wisdom is that?" (James 3: 15–18). Such wisdom does not come from heaven, but is earthly, non-spiritual, and of the devil. Where you have envy and selfish ambition, there you find disorder and every evil practice, but the wisdom that comes from heaven is, first of all, pure and then peace-loving, considerate, submissive, full of mercy and good fruit, impartial, and sincere.

Peacemakers who sow in peace raise a harvest of righteousness. History has demonstrated down through the centuries what happens when nations and the people reject God's Holy Word—they end up in a cesspool of wickedness. Just take a quick glance at our own nation, which is backsliding, progressively stumbling into sins of all kinds from abortion to same-sex marriages and idolatrous behaviorism almost beyond belief. Yes, that is indeed a complete revelation of the level of wisdom that rejects the Word of God!

Yes, dear reader, Jeremiah grieved deeply because of the destruction of Jerusalem and the devastation of his nation. But in the depths of his grief, there shined a ray of hope. God's compassion is forever present. His faithfulness is magnificent. Jeremiah realized that it is only God's mercy that has prevented total annihilation. He showed us the serious consequences of sin and how we can always have hope in the midst of tragedy because God is able to turn it around for good. We are well aware of the power of prayer and of our need for the repentance of sin. We all face tragedies in our lives, yes, but in the midst of our difficulties, there is hope in God.

Dear friend, as one of God's most heroic and courageous prophets, Jeremiah stood alone in the depth of his emotions, broken by the care for his people, his love for the nation, and his devotion to God. Personally, I am not ashamed of the tears that I have quite often shed. How about you? Do you weep because your selfish pride has been injured, because the loved ones around you are leading sinful lives, or because they have rejected the God who loves them so dearly? Do you shed tears over something you have lost, or because your loved ones will suffer for their sinfulness?

Think about it, our own nation is filled with injustice, poverty, perverseness, and rebellion against God, all of which should move us to tears—and to action! It is true, the people have much to cry about because of their rebellion against God, but was this suffering God's fault? No! It was due to their sinful ways. Their suffering should bring them to the Lord, weeping for forgiveness. If we cry out to God in repentance, He will forgive us.

Like most Christians, you will probably admit that God loves you, but do you think He likes you? Or do you think He merely puts up with you because, after all, His Son died for you? Dear reader, our Heavenly Father desires to have fellowship with each of us. He desires our love, even while we are sinning. In Romans 5: 8, Paul says, "But God demonstrates His own love for us in this: While we were still sinners, Christ died for us!" Let us have these words sink deeply into our hearts; otherwise, we will never be free from the guilt that accompanies sin. The plan that secured our forgiveness was God's idea: He initiated it, and He wants us for His very own. Jeremiah saw the intense suffering of God's people. He never questioned God's justice in sending this suffering. Instead, he celebrated God's faithfulness and His unfailing love.

Let's you and I concentrate on how Jesus suffered to pay the penalty for our sins and let us rejoice in the incredible love of the God who offers us salvation. Wisdom tells us that we may have a personal loving relationship with the eternal God through faith in Jesus Christ. Christ Himself must become the focal point of our entire life. As King David said, "Even though I walk through the valley of the shadow of death…you are with me."

In that relationship with God experienced by men and women just like ourselves, we will find the focal point that absolutely no experience in life can ever destroy. This is the wonderful wisdom in His Word.

> Redemption can be yours since Christ broke the bread,
> Through the wine His mercy immerses your soul,
> Sinners need no longer their tears to shed,
> In His holy communion we were made whole.
>
> By His grace our spirit is now being fed,
> The Last Supper reveals how He died in our place,
> His Word points to Calvary where our Savior bled—
> To prepare us for eternity—to meet Him face to face!
>
> —Russell Young

Daniel

In the book of Daniel, we shall learn that Daniel was the last of the so-called Major Prophets. To me, Daniel's tremendous courage, honor, loyalty to God, and magnificent God-given wisdom always take my heart back to the patriarch, Joseph. Under King Epiphanes, we see efforts to lead the faithful in Jerusalem to abandon their practice of living by the Laws of Moses and to stop their temple worship. This king partially destroyed Jerusalem by ravishing the city and the temple sanctuary and made it virtually impossible to hold services of worship there at all. As a result, many Jews gave up their religion and turned to the pagan religion of the king.

In the very first chapter of the book of Daniel, we learn that he was carried away into captivity to Babylon as a young boy. He never returned to Jerusalem, and yet (like Joseph) he came to occupy positions of power. In the kingdoms of Babylon, Media, and Persia, he was held captive without ever turning away from the unswerving loyalty to the God of his fathers. Daniel, with his devoted friends who had adopted the Babylonian names of Meshach, Shadrach, and Abednego, made every effort to keep their fellow Jews loyal to the traditions of their fathers, even at the cost of martyrdom. They believed, as we shall observe, that in a brief time their troubles would be over, the tyrant would be dead, and the happy age of deliverance and victory for the Jewish people would come. As a matter of fact, Daniel, time and again, desired to impress upon the hearts of the Jewish people that the ultimate triumph of the kingdom of God was near. The book of Daniel directs us to the idea of a heavenly kingdom, which later appears in a more clearly developed form in the New Testament.

Daniel, meanwhile, teaching about angels, shows them appearing in a more definite form, influencing the lives of people and nations and determining their destinies. Angels were given names for the first time—Michael (guardian angel) and Gabriel (heaven-sent interpreter). Also, perhaps, even more significantly, a reference is made to the resurrection in Daniel 12: 2–4: "Multitudes who sleep in the dust of the earth will awake: some to everlasting life, others to everlasting shame and everlasting contempt. Those who are wise will shine like the brightness of the Heavens, and those who lead many to righteousness, like the stars forever and ever. But you, Daniel, close up and seal the words of the scroll until the time of the end. Many will go here and there to increase knowledge."

Oh, how often I have spoken about "how time flies!" At my age of eighty-five, I often wonder, where did it all go? How quickly my life has gone by! We simply are not used to that thing called *time*. We are not adjusted to it, and we cannot comprehend it. This, at least in my mind, is absolute proof that eternity does exist and that it is our future home. Yes, dear reader, Daniel's influence has been widespread and thoroughly bolstered by his extensive wisdom. In fact, the faith of the Jewish people has been kept alive down through the centuries through wars, poverty, slavery, and distress through crisis after crisis by the prophetic words of Daniel. Even to this very day, his words have served you and me in times of emergencies and calamities by assuring us of the ultimate triumph of the kingdom of God.

Take into your heart these words of our Lord and Savior Jesus Christ from the Book of Matthew 24:12–17: "Because of the increase of wickedness, the love of most will grow cold, but he who stands firm to the end will besaved. And this Gospel of the Kingdom will be preached in the whole world as a testimony to all nations, and then the end will come. So when you see standing in the Holy place the abomination that causes desolation, spoken of through the prophet Daniel, let the reader understand, then let those who are in Judea flee to the mountains." Yes, those prophetic words of Daniel, reiterated by Jesus, are meant to prepare us for the Second Coming. This exemplifies and brings forth the God-given wisdom of Daniel. Indeed, he came to occupy positions of power in Babylon, Media, and Persia without ever wavering or deflecting from his loyalty to the God of our fathers. He was among the men selected for the royal service and entered into a working relationship with the high court from the very beginning. He learned the ways of the captors, as well as their language, in order to be placed in a position next to the king.

Daniel's character never deteriorated throughout his life. The secret of his strength was his solid faith, along with the steady conviction of willpower that he possessed. He asked of the king that he have permission to live and to act according to that conviction. God acted on his behalf, and his request was granted! Write that gift on the tablet of your heart. God is always in cooperation, ready and willing to control circumstances in the interest of those of faith.

Dear friend, God is all-knowing, and He is in charge of our lives. He will overcome evil and deliver the faithful. Our faith is secure because our future is secure in Jesus Christ. Daniel was dedicated and committed, determined to serve God regardless of the outcome. You and I must disobey anyone who would ask us to disobey God. Look at how God was faithful in Daniel's life. He delivered Daniel from execution, from a lion's den, and from enemies who hated him. God cares for you and deals patiently with us at all times. Therefore, let us always remain faithful to Him.

As an excellent case in point, I would refer you to Daniel 2:16–18: "At this, Daniel went into the King and asked for time, so that he might interpret the dream for him. Then Daniel returned to his house and explained the matter to his friends, Shadrach, Meshach, and Abednego. He urged them to pray for mercy from the God of Heaven concerning this mystery, so that he and his friends might not be executed with the rest of the wise men of Babylon." Daniel went to his friends, and they prayed. This is a beautiful example of how like-minded people living in loving loyalty to God should turn to God in prayer. The prayer was heard and answered. There is no force that is as powerful as prayer to keep one not only safe but also productive in God's service. This is especially true when it is strengthened by the fellowship and comradeship of fellow souls in communication with the Almighty God. Prayer confirms, solidifies, and verifies your hope in God. Daniel's prayer was answered, and he immediately took time to give God credit for all power and wisdom and thanked God for answering his prayer.

Dear friend, how do you feel when your prayers are answered? Be like Daniel. Accompany your loving prayers with thankfulness when those prayers are answered. Whatever may be your desire, whatever your needs, always thank God for His wisdom. Read in James 1:5: "If any of you lack wisdom, he should ask God, who gives generously to all without finding fault, and it will be given to him."

For the past several years, I have been praying for another Billy Graham. Right here in our First United

Methodist Church of Van Wert, Ohio, in just a few short years, we have lost by death four pillars of strength from our church—Herb Kephart, Roy Souders, Bob Scheidt, and Walter Harris. Throughout the world, we are losing such outstanding men of God. I think of an old country song, "Who's Gonna Fill Their Shoes." Let us all join together in prayer, asking God to send more men of honor, loyalty, and wisdom—such as Daniel—into our midst. God will provide.

My wonderful friend, Wayne Compton, knows the answer to our worldly dilemma and explains it in just one word: love. Let us all, through the love of Christ, pray for a world that will turn to God and to one another in love. As we just read in the Book of James, "If you lack wisdom, ask God." I ask you to look closely at the life of Daniel. He maintained a close and loving personal relationship with God. He walked side by side in Holy righteousness with his Heavenly Father at all times. Not just when he felt a specific need, but at all hours, all the days of his life. My friend, this led Daniel directly to the source of his honor, his loyalty, his devotional strength, his unwavering faith, and finally to his God-given wisdom.

Even in this great nation, our own United States of America, we find so many people trying to be stars in the world of entertainment, only to find that stardom is not merely temporary, but so often mentally and physically destructive. God leads us into eternal stardom by means of holy righteousness, our divine wisdom, and our sharing of the Lord with others. Yes, we will go through difficult times, but these times will purify us if we will accept and learn from them. We read in the Book of Romans 3:5: "Not only so, also rejoice in our suffering, because we know that suffering produces perseverance, perseverance character, and character hope. And hope does not disappoint us, because God has poured out His love into our hearts by the Holy Spirit, whom He has given us."

Dear reader, our hope is in the resurrected Jesus Christ. The Book of Daniel 12:12 begins with "Blessed is the one who waits…" You and I both know many Christians who live in a constant state of anxiety, fretting and raging as they go. To be perfectly at peace is a secret worth knowing. What is the use of worrying? No one becomes stronger by worrying. Worrying never helped anyone be a better servant of God. Worry doesn't help you escape from your difficulties. Worry actually spoils lives, which otherwise would be useful and attractive.

Our Lord forbids worry. He said, "Take no thought about what we shall eat, or what we drink, or how shall we be clothed." We are not to worry about these things because the anxiety shows in your face, in your voice, the way you walk, and in your overall lack of a jubilant spirit. Oh, be still and know that Jehovah is God. Recognize and give into the fact that His every Word will stand, regardless of our frustrations in life. He deserves to be confided in.

Put your trust in Jesus Christ always and wait in His glorious wisdom. Do not be shouting that the sun is destroyed when it becomes cloudy; the sun is still there, and summer is on its way. Remember, April showers bring May flowers.

When God hides His face, do not say that He has forgotten you. Waiting builds grace and strengthens our faith, so wait in hope. His promise is for you, so wait and fret not. My dear mother often told us as we left the house that a sparrow told a robin that he wondered why people rushed about and worried so much. Well, the robin told the sparrow that they probably didn't have a Heavenly Father that looks after people like the one that cared for them.

Psalm 37:1 reads, "Fret not..." I have found in counseling sessions on anger control and on anxieties in general that each person who had sought God's help in the understanding and solution of his or her anger without exception received that help. They described the result as miraculous! There is, for sure, a miracle involved. It is the miracle of God's love for us, the miracle of His redeeming grace.

In Isaiah 30:18, it says, "Therefore will the Lord wait, that He may be gracious unto thee!" The Lord is watching over you in your stressful situation, and He will come gloriously to your help. Do not grieve Him by doubting His love. In fact, you should raise your head and begin to praise Him now for the deliverance that is on the way to you, and you will be glorified for the waiting that tried your faith.

Dear reader, the Lord said through the prophet Daniel, "Blessed is he that waiteth." I realize, as you do also, that it may sound easy to wait, but it isn't always that easy. However, let us wait in prayer. Call upon God and tell Him of your problem and plead for His promise to help. Wait in faith. Tell Him of your confidence in Him. Believe that even though He is causing you to wait, He will come, so wait in quiet patience, saying simply, "Thy will be done." Remember the old German proverb: "Patience is a bitter plant, but it has a sweet fruit!" Yes, we are impatient people, even those of us who claim to be Christians. We have so many responsibilities, busy schedules, and well-planned goals to be met, but patience is a virtue that always has the future in mind. Romans 8:25 tells us, "If we hope for what we do not have, we wait for it patiently." If we want to be people of patience, we must trust that God is in control of our future. What we call a detour just might be the Lord's more scenic route.

I am reminded of a trip my wife and I made a few years ago. We had driven through Italy, and we were headed to Switzerland. We had reservations for the night in Geneva, and we were making good time. All of a sudden, we ran into a detour outside of Geneva, and our timing was in jeopardy. Anxiety and frustration began to set in. We drove on the detoured route for twenty-seven miles. Was this a cause for concern? Perhaps, but it was around the beautiful Lake Geneva, and I would venture to say that it was the most wonderful scenery that we had beholden on the entire European tour. Without that detour, we would have missed the blessing, and we still got to our hotel on time!

As the prophet Daniel recommended, if we will wait, we people of patience must trust in God's control of the outcome. When our plans are delayed, when our timing is interrupted, when our goals are being frustrated, God still knows the best way home. Wait upon His wisdom, and He shall lead you into His eternal abode. Daniel, writing from Babylon during the time of exile, wants us to know that God controls everything and that the victory belongs to the Lord and to those who do His will. Even the pagan kings in Babylon must admit this truth. Let us all think about how God controls our lives and how we will win out over the forces of evil when we obey the Lord. Through the prophet Jeremiah, God said, "'I know the plans I have for you,' declares the Lord, 'Plans to prosper you and not to harm you, plans to give you hope and a future.'"

Dear friend, God calls it hope, and it is from Him we learn that when all else seems dim, it is hope, along with faith and love, that will persist. Finally, Daniel received this message from God: "As for you, go your way til the end. You will rest, and then at the end of the days you will arise to receive your allotted inheritance." Dear reader, in the words of the great Alfred Lord Tennyson, "Strong Son of God, immortal love…we have not seen thy face, by faith, and faith alone embrace, believing where we cannot prove."

Paul says in Romans 15:13, "May the God of hope fill you with all joy and peace as you trust in Him so that you may overflow with hope by the power of the Holy Spirit." Daniel received once again the promise of resurrection. He would one day see the fulfillment of God's promise. He rested in the comfort of God's power and looked forward to the time when he would rise and receive eternal life with the Master.

In our lifetime, God does not reveal everything that we shall encounter. We must accept what He gives us to see. In His own time, God will tell us all we need to know. The power of trust results in our ability to turn over the control of our lives to Him who knows more about the future than we ever will. Trust in the way of utmost wisdom. As the prophet Daniel told us, our trust in God gives us the power to act with courage and to forgive with pleasure. Our trust in Him gives us the power to stand strong in repentance, in obedience, and in compassion, along with tolerance and respect. Through trust and hope, we gain the power to commit our future to the most Holy One who sees the path around the bend. Your wisdom will deliver you.

Finally, my friend, I can assume that by now you can see why the prophet Daniel reminds me so much of the patriarch, Joseph They were truly men of great honor, courage, and loyalty to God. Their close loving relationship with God was evident in their everyday lives. Both great men walked in righteousness, and their strong, diligent faith produced the wisdom that was so magnificently exemplified in their service to the Almighty Father. It was through strong and devoted faithfulness that Daniel was dedicated to keeping his fellow Jews loyal to the traditions of their fathers, even at the cost of martyrdom. By his consecrated faithfulness, he accepted the seemingly impossible task given to him, and he performed superbly in the manifestation of doing God's holy will.

Let us read Daniel 5:13–17:

> Daniel was brought before the king, and the king said to him, "Are you Daniel, one of the exiles my father, the king, brought from Judah? I have heard that the spirit of the gods is in you and that you have insight, intelligence, along with outstanding wisdom. The wise men, and enchanters were brought before me to read this writing and tell me what it means, but they could not explain it. Now, I have heard that you are able to give explanations, and to solve difficult problems. If you can read this writing, and tell me what it means, you will be clothed in purple and have a gold chain placed around your neck, and you will bemade the third highest ruler in the kingdom." Then Daniel answered the king, "You may keep your gifts for yourself, and give your rewards to someone else. Nevertheless, I will read the writing for the king and tell him what it means."

Well, here we go again. Daniel has been in this spot before. In fact, the king, at that time, had ordered everyone who had failed to interpret his dream to be executed. Daniel was the only one with a true God to consult, and he was the only one brave enough to give the king a discouraging report. Daniel's past spiritual experiences in interpreting dreams had given him strength to build on his spiritual powers. This tells us that we too, by listening to God's urgings and pleadings with us, can grow to be accustomed to the sound of His voice. Please notice, Daniel was not motivated by material rewards. Throughout his entire life, he had sought always to do what was right before the Lord. He wanted the king to know that his interpretation of the dream was true and unadulterated.

Doing what is right should always be our motivation, regardless of any rewards whatsoever. I ask you, my friend, do you love God enough to do what is right in spite of losses that may come your way? Each of us must stand before our Heavenly Father and give an account of our lives. Therefore, I plead with you to live each day of your life fully aware that you will one day appear before God. How will your life measure up? I pray that God will say to you, "Well done, good and faithful servant. Enter into the kingdom.

In Daniel, we have an excellent example of a life well lived. Daniel quietly and faithfully performed his duties in whatever he did and wherever he was He never considered for disobedience or insubordination. If you are truly seeking to be a spiritual child of God, strong in faith and filled with His wisdom, then emulate the life of God's prophet Daniel.

> Lord Jesus, as I kneel in this quiet place,
> I plead for your fulfilling grace,
> In this solemn evening hour,
> I seek the fullness of your power,
> May I, in every moment of daily living,
> Show your mercies through my forgiving,
> And when my days on earth are done,
> May I hear, "Welcome home, my faithful son!"
>
> —Russell Young

Matthew

Matthew was one of Jesus's twelve devoted disciples. Once he was a despised tax collector, but his life was changed by the man from Galilee. Matthew wrote this Gospel to his fellow Jews to prove that Jesus is the Messiah and to explain God's kingdom. Matthew wrote this Gospel to emphasize how Jesus fulfills God's promises from the Old Testament. He includes numerous sayings of Jesus about living as one of His disciples and as a member of the church. He concludes with the call of Jesus that we make disciples of all nations.

I would ask you to sincerely ask yourself if you are living as a disciple of Jesus, and how well you are telling others about the life of Jesus. I must point out that more than four hundred years had passed since the last Old Testament prophecies, and faithful Jews all over the world were still waiting for the Messiah. Matthew wrote this book to Jews to present Jesus as King and Messiah, the promised descendant of David who would reign forever. You will find as you read these words about the Gospel of Matthew that they show the link between the Old Testament and the New Testament, and especially demonstrate how Jesus fulfilled the Old Testament prophecies.

Dear reader, I feel that I should say something about the church as I see it today. I am quite sure that anybody who has a spiritually sensitive soul is a bit disturbed. It seems to me that the attitude today displays an "easygoing" Christianity. We do not seem to know the true meaning of discipleship. As a matter of fact, I have recently read these words concerning our attitude in the church today: "Millions of Christians live in a sentimental haze of vague piety, with soft organ music trembling in the lovely light from stained glass windows. Their religion is a thing of pleasant emotional quivers, divorced from the realities, divorced from the intellect, and demanding little except lip service to a few harmless platitudes." I will say from the depths of my heart that I detest that kind of Christianity, and, God being my Helper, I will do what I can to change that easygoing Christianity to lead my fellow Christians into a mode of true Christian discipleship. Will you join me?

In Matthew 16:14–27, we read very clearly the demands of the Lord from us, His children. He speaks boldly and clearly, saying exactly what we must do in order to attain discipleship. "If any man would come after me, let him deny himself and take up his cross, and follow me. Look at it this way: Christ said, "Deny thyself," here you have two possibilities—*pity* thyself, *deny* thyself. Only the second one is Christian. Satan would have us pity ourselves, but Christ demands that we deny ourselves.

My friend, let us face the fact: the Christian life is not a picnic nor a joyride to heaven. Yes, we will have difficulties, and, yes, we will have hardships to encounter when we follow Him. Deny thyself. Take up the cross. Remember, your cross is what you suffer because you are a Christian. Yield yourself to the will of God.

In the Book of Matthew, the all-commanding figure that maintains our attention and captures our imagination is none other than Jesus of Nazareth. He is the incomparable teacher of divine truth and the wonderful healer of disease and sickness. His human life was completely dedicated to the service of mankind. People, just like ourselves, heard His message with great joy, but the religious leaders with tragic blindness and finally with a crucifixion. No one can read through the words of wisdom found in the writings of Matthew without being moved to praise and prompted to worship in spirit and in truth.

Interestingly, we know little about Matthew himself. We do know that he was a tax collector and that he must have been a bitterly hated man since the Jews hated members of their own race who worked in the service of their conquerors. There was, however, one special gift that Matthew possessed. Most of the disciples had been fishermen and had very little skill in the art of writing. Matthew had great skill and the expertise of putting words to paper, helped along with spiritual wisdom.

When Jesus called Matthew, he rose up and followed Him using his literary skill to become the first man ever to put together the works and the teachings of Jesus. There are certain traits in Matthew's Gospel that must be pointed out. First, it was written for the Jews. One of Matthew's greatest tasks was to demonstrate that all of the prophecies of the Old Testament are fulfilled in Jesus, and so He must be the Messiah. A phrase that occurs sixteen times in Matthew's Gospel is "All this was done that it might be fulfilled, which was spoken to the prophet…" Matthew's main desire was to show how the Old Testament prophecies received their fulfillment in Jesus. In this Gospel, every detail of Jesus life was spoken of by the prophets, and so it was that the Jews had to admit that Jesus was the Messiah.

Yes, Matthews's main interest was in the Jews. However, we are not to think that the Gospel in any way excludes the Gentiles. For instance, in Matthew 24:14, we read, "The Gospel is to be preached to the whole world." And again, Matthew says to all of us in the church in chapter 28 verse 19, "Go ye therefore and teach all nations." Yes, he was definitely interested in the church. By the time the Book of Matthew was written, the church had become the dominant factor in the life of the Christian. Matthew also had a strong interest in the End Times—God's Judgment, referring often to the Second Coming, as in chapter 25 verses 31 to 46, "The Sheep and The Goats!" Matthew, in the very first chapter, stressed two major points about Jesus. He stressed the fact that Jesus was the son of David. In fact, the average, ordinary, common Jew referred to Jesus as the son of David.

The Jews had been waiting for a son of David to lead them to the glory that was to come. They never could forget that they were the chosen people of God. Yes, they suffered through a long period of disasters, captivity, even slavery, but they never forgot the coming victory. Jesus was the answer to their dreams. However, some didn't understand. Could we possibly say the same thing about many people today? Many see their dreams in power, wealth, materialism, and status. You and I, along with other fully believing Christians, know that all of our dreams can only be realized in the Savior and Redeemer, our Lord Jesus Christ.

Matthew also stressed that Jesus fulfilled all prophecies—that is, the message of the prophets came true through Christ—and by doing so, he declared that this is a planned universe with purpose and design and that God is in control. Matthew's wisdom shines through as he teaches us that our lives and the entire creation of the world are on the way to the goal that God has arranged.

Early on in the Book of Matthew, we learned how we can display God's wisdom in our daily lives. Mathew 4:1 says, "Then Jesus was led by the Spirit into the wilderness to be tempted by the devil." Let us examine an important word used in that verse. It is vital that we understand the meaning of the word *tempt*. In our language, the word *tempt* has a bad meaning. It means to entice someone to do wrong, to try to seduce someone to do wrong, to try to seduce them to sin, or to travel down the wrong path. In Hebrew, the word is *peirazein*, meaning "to test." Rather than "to tempt," the word actually means "to test."

Remember Genesis 22:1: "And, it came to pass after these things that God did tempt Abraham." God would never lead anyone into wrongdoing. The verse, if to be understood correctly, should read, "And it came to pass after these things that God *tested* Abraham." The time had arrived for Abraham to be tested for his loyalty to God.

And so, let us examine it in another light: what we call temptation is not meant to call us to sin; rather, it is meant to enable us to defeat sin, not to make us bad, but to make us good. Therefore, let us think of the verse as meaning Jesus was being tested, not tempted, in His wilderness experience. Jesus went into the wilderness to be alone. His work had been laid out for him. God had spoken to Jesus, and Jesus was considering how He would complete the task. And so, to get things straight in His mind before beginning the work, Jesus went into the wilderness to be alone.

I ask you, my friend, could it be that we often go wrong because we simply do not try to be alone? There are certain things that require to be worked out alone, times when no one else's advice is needed, and times to stop acting and to start thinking. Wisdom does inform us that we make mistakes when we do give ourselves a chance to be alone with God.

Think of it—the only person who could have ever told of this event was Jesus Himself. He was in the wilderness alone. No one was with Him as He went through the testing time. It is to us that Jesus is baring His heart and soul. He is saying to us that He can help others who are being tested because He Himself was tested. Jesus answered the tester (Satan) with these words, "You shall worship the Lord your God, and Him alone you will serve." Let this be our reply, "Where you lead me, Lord, I shall follow. Wherever you go, I shall go."

There is another interesting side to this event of being tested by our Father through suffering. A few years ago, I was touring in Italy and came across a pottery plant that was producing chinaware. The pieces were all laid out and painted, ready for the oven. I noticed that they were anything but attractive. The paint was drab, a reddish color, very dull- and messy-looking. You look at it and you say, "Wow, who would ever buy something like that?" Then, it is put in the fire. Later it is put in the fire again. And then once again, it went into the fire. Three times in the fire, and when that china came out of the last firing, there was a luster, a glow of red. The black around the edge was a shining gold that would last for generations...It only became that way because of the fire. The paint, which was previously smudged and smeared, was now absolutely fast. It is burnt into the china. It is now of great value because of the fire.

That is what God does with you. Are you blessed? Then He will burn the blessing in. He blesses you by testing you, that you may learn by the heat of the trial, and you have come rejoicing because of your victory. He has proven once again that He loves you. Now, go back and get ready for more testing. Do you know why? Because God has shown you, "My grace is sufficient for you." Now that you have experienced it, He will put you back on His grace alone.

Now, suddenly the suffering seems to be more severe, and though the blessing of the Holy Spirit has come upon you, it seems like the Spirit is doing nothing but driving you back into the wilderness. He is there with all of His grace, and once again He is sufficient. You ask, why was the devil allowed to test our Savior? Why does the devil test you? Matthew tells us that "Christ was tested right up to the very end of His life." In fact, Christ was made perfect through suffering and testing. The fact that you are being tested, the Bible says, proves that you are a child of God.

I am sure you have learned, as I have, that when everything is easy, you have no problems. It is easy to forget God, right? Well, fire and testing keep us pure, deepen our fellowship with the Lord, and, in the testing and the pressure, we are driven back to Him. It does strengthen our faith. So, when testing comes, we shout, "Hallelujah!" In James 1:2, we read, "Count it all joy when you fall into diverse testing." Jesus was victor in the wilderness and throughout His life, tested in all points, just as we are, and yet He was without sin. Yes, Christ, the risen and resurrected Lord ascended into victory, and He means for you and me to also have victory.

What is the secret to being victorious? Let us examine three essentials for victory. First, search the scriptures and know the Word of God—His Wisdom is to be found in His Word! Then, get into fasting. Matthew 9: 29 says, "Victory comes through prayer and fasting." This fasting helps you to maintain a disciplined body. The Apostle Paul wrote, "I buffet myself, I keep under my body." In addition to scriptures and to fasting, we have to worship. "It is written, thou shalt worship the Lord thy God, and Him only thou shalt serve." Worship includes more than prayer and adoration; it also includes meditation and intercession. Worship is waiting and dwelling in the holiest with the Lord. Have you noticed that our Lord found it necessary to go to God's house? "He went to the synagogue on the Sabbath day, as was His custom."

Also, my dear friend, be on the attack. "If you want to make the devil run, pop him with the Gospel gun!" Get out and tell others of the Savior. Be active in the Lord's work. That is vital so that when the devil comes, he will find you attacking.

Finally, as you play your part, as you are out there actively in service, as you are going on in the Word of God, as you are living close to the Lord in prayer and in worship, my friend, go forth with Him who is victorious. "He is able to keep you from stumbling and to present you faultless before the throne of His glory with exceeding joy." Dear reader, wisdom tells us to say yes to God, so that even though you say no to the greatest ambitions that you have and to those choice desires that you have, you are still God's disciple: you deny yourself. You say yes to Christ and follow Him. Would you think about this with me? Why should we, who are children of God, do what the Lord Jesus asks of us? Well, immediately I would say to you—He gave His all, how can we do less for Him who gave His all?

However, throughout His Holy Word, we find His reasons are sufficient. "For whosoever would save his life, shall lose it; and whosoever shall lose his life for my sake, shall find it." Notice that it is not grasping and getting things for ourselves, finding ease and comfort, and pitying ourselves that are going to allow us to really live. It is the giving of ourselves to the Lord Jesus, handing over our lives to Him, by losing our life that we find it.

Another reason is this: "What shall a man be profited if he shall gain the whole world, and forfeit his life? And what shall a man give in exchange for his life?" By following the Lord Jesus Christ, you are making the most profitable use of the life span that God has given you. I don't care how much money, stocks, and bonds you have, or how famous you are. My friend, your most valuable possessions are those days and weeks, those months and years that God has given you down here. Pray, "Lord, teach me the value of these hours!" Discipleship is living. It means that you are using your time on earth to the best possible advantage.

Dear reader, "Deny yourself, take up your cross, and follow me. For the Son of Man shall come in the glory of the Father, with His angels, and then shall He render unto every man according to his deeds." Yes, we are going to give an answer someday as to how we use this precious time He has given us. These are words of wisdom to live by. My friend, discipleship means we really live, not just exist or kill time, but truly live with all of the throbbing, pulsating quality of real life. It means that when we stand at the judgment seat of Christ, we shall not have to be ashamed. Yes, dear reader, your spiritually sensitive soul has seen enough of that easygoing, laid-back, watered down so-called Christianity we see in America today. Let us, with God's help, dedicate ourselves to a life of true discipleship and step forward as a mighty nation of devoted followers obedient to the call of Christ. "If any man will come after me, let him deny himself and take up his cross and follow me." This is the wisdom of the Word at work in the world.

The Old Testament prophecies and genealogies in the Book of Matthew present Jesus's credentials for being king of the world—not a military or political leader, as the disciples had originally hoped. Rather than a military or political leader, Jesus was the spiritual king sent from the Father to overcome all evil and rule in the hearts of all people. If we refuse to serve the King faithfully, we are disloyal followers who are fit only to be banished from the kingdom. Let each of us make Jesus king of our lives and worship Him as our Savior, King, and Lord.

Heavenly Father, I do surrender everything unto you who died for me. I now ask you to accept my tenderhearted prayer. I am asking that as long as I follow you, you take my heart and let it be placed forever before your throne. Now here on bended knee, I do promise to live for you forever. Teach me, Lord, that I may understand what it is that you would have me do. Give me wisdom that I may grow ever closer to you, and that I may always glorify your Holy Spirit. Fill me, Lord, with your Divine Word, and give me strength to abide in it. Amen.

Mark

John Mark, the author of this book, was not one of the twelve disciples. He did, however, go with the Apostle Paul on his first missionary journey. We must agree with the Bible scholars who say that the Book of Mark may just be the most important in the world, and that is said because it is the earliest of all the Gospels and the first writings of the life of Jesus to come down to us. We can also say it is the first writings of the life of Jesus that has survived. Also, it is obvious that Matthew and Luke had Mark's writings in hand as they wrote their Gospels.

John Mark was the son of a wealthy lady named Mary who lived in Jerusalem, and her house was an important meeting place of the early church. Mark was brought up in the very midst of Christian fellowship. Many times he heard people tell of their personal memories of Jesus. After all, Mark was Peter's interpreter. Mark had not heard, nor did he follow Jesus, but he followed Peter later on and recorded the events and words of Christ taken from the disciples. So then, we have two great reasons why Mark is a very important Book. First, as we have learned, it is the earliest of all the Gospels. Second, it contains the record of what Peter preached and taught about Jesus. In fact, it is as close as we can ever get to having an eyewitness account of the life of Jesus.

Mark's writing on the life of Jesus did not begin with His birth, or even with John the Baptist in the wilderness. It began with the prophets long ago. In Mark 1:2–3, it is written in the Book of Isaiah the prophet: "I will send my messenger ahead of you, who will prepare your way." In other words, it all began with the Almighty God! Ancient Greek philosophers believed in the arranged plan of God. One of them said, "The things of God are full of foresight. All things flow from heaven." Yes, wisdom does flow from heaven. It is an honor to help in this great process that is actively being completed by our Father in heaven who sees the end from the beginning. Wouldn't our lives be so much more exciting, let alone enjoyable, if we could all get together and bring God's ultimate goal closer to its ultimate end?

The goal will never be reached unless people, such as you and me, will work to make it possible. It is an often proven fact that where Christ is allowed to enter, the miraculous Christian faith cleanses the sinful, immoral society and leaves it pure and clean. Begin with those near you. Many of us have beloved family members that we are praying for on a daily basis.

The family may be the most difficult place to be a witness for Jesus. Your faith may be misinterpreted as criticism. Your zeal may be misunderstood. You may have been accused of being a hypocrite because other areas of your life still fall short of Christ's ideals. Uncommitted people may view your commitment to the Bible as unreasonable bigotry. Family members require the most patience. They see us at our worst when our guard is down. Remember, Christ's family rejected and ridiculed Him. Jesus knows what you face by trying to be a witness for Him in your own family. Try always to stay true to your faith. Do not get upset and attack those who are aggressively putting you down. Over time, your love for your family will bring a positive effect. "Take it to the Lord in prayer!"

It is clear that the ministry of John the Baptist was greatly effective. They flocked out to listen to him and to be baptized. What caused him to be so effective? My friend, John was a man who lived his message, and not only his words, but also his life, demonstrated his protest against the worldly way of living. He was effective because he told people what in their hearts they already knew and what they had wanted deep down in their souls; yes, what they had been longing for.

John's message was effective because he pointed to something and someone higher than they. John's one aim was not to be the center of attraction, but to connect people to the "one" whom all men need. Mark 1: 5 says, "And the whole country of Judea went out to him, and so did all of the people of Jerusalem, and they were baptized by him in the Jordan River, while they confessed their sins!"

My dear friend, John's baptism was a baptism of repentance meant for those who were sorry for their sins and who wanted to show their determination to be done with them. In other words, it was decision time. We are aware of the fact that the undecided life is the wasted life, the frustrated life, the discontented life, and many times the tragic life. Words of wisdom—heed them well.

To each of us, a way is opened, and the decision is sure to take us to the road we shall follow. Some are apt to take the low road to sin and destruction. Others will take the higher road, the road that leads to Jesus Christ and on into heaven to our eternal abode. In Mark 1:15, after John was put in prison, Jesus went into Galilee, proclaiming the good news of God. "'The time has come,' He said, 'The Kingdom of God is near. REPENT and believe the good news!'"

I capitalized the word *repent* in order to gain emphasis. The Greek word for it is *metanoia*, which means "a change of mind." Yes, many people are sorry for the consequences of their sin and are sorry for them. Yet, we know that many people, if they could escape the consequences, would continue in the same sinful ways. They do not hate the sins; it is the consequences that they hate.

Words of wisdom from 1 John 1:6–9: "If we claim to have fellowship with Him, yet walk in darkness, we lie and do not live by truth. But if we walk in the light, as He is in the light, we have fellowship with one another, and the blood of Jesus, His Son, purifies us from all sin. If we claim to be without sin, we deceive ourselves and the truth is not in us. If we confess our sins, He is faithful and just, and He will forgive our sins and purify us from all unrighteousness." "*If* we confess our sins…" The biggest word in scripture just might be that two-letter word—*if*. For confessing sins—admitting failure—is exactly what our pride refuses to do. To mourn for your sins is natural when you are lacking in spirit. Beatitudes—"Blessed are the poor in spirit… Blessed are they who mourn."

Many people deny their weaknesses. Many people know they are wrong, and yet pretend they are right. Therefore, they never taste the beautiful sorrow of repentance. Of all of the paths to pure joy, this one has to be the strongest. True blessedness, as Jesus says, begins with deep sadness. Wisdom tells us, "Blessed are those who know they are in trouble, and have enough sense to admit it!"

You and I both recognize the fact that all of us regard our failures as understandable mistakes when, if we were honest about it, we would admit we have made inexcusably selfish choices. We know that excuse-making has been a natural tendency in people ever since Adam blamed Eve and Eve blamed the snake. If we were not leaning on

185

our self-justification, we would be forced to face ourselves squarely as we really are—corrupt by God's standards and deserving of punishment. I wonder if we are actually capable of seeing ourselves as condemned sinners, worthy of judgment, powerless to improve ourselves, humbled by a lack of defense, and totally at the mercy of a righteous and angry judge. I ask you, my friend, does that sound like joy to you? How could joy emerge from such misery? Wisdom tells us that this painful plight of humility and powerlessness, followed by judgment, is not only where life begins, but also where joy surges ahead in its heavenly growth.

Dear reader, this predicament that we find ourselves in is not unique to us. Seneca, one of the greatest philosophers of all time, wrote, "God is near you, with you, within you. A Holy Spirit sits within us, spectator of our evil and of our good and our guardian. Man's part in life is to be the interpreter of God. Man is the son of God, and his duty is to attach himself to God and, like a soldier, to obey God's signals and commands. He is to look up to God and say, "Use me for whatever you will!"

And today, we shall read from Mark 8:34–35: "Then He called the crowd to Him along with His disciples and said, "If anyone would come after me, he must deny himself and take up his cross and follow me. For whoever wants to save his life will lose it, but whoever loses his life for me and for the Gospel will save it."

Those, my friend, are words of wisdom from the Master Himself. Jesus is calling us into discipleship that will free us from our man-made dilemmas, from our anxieties, from every oppressive burden that afflicts us. We must submit to the loving yoke of Jesus Christ. We must finally face the fact that we can only obtain freedom and enjoy His fellowship by following Him and accepting His call to discipleship. The command of Jesus is hard for those who try to resist it, but for those who willingly submit, the yoke is easy, and the burden is light. His command is not like a spiritual shock treatment. Jesus never asks for anything without giving us the strength to do it. He never wants to destroy life, but to promote life, to strengthen and heal it.

Dear reader, I am proud to say that I served in the United States Army in World War II in Italy. I heard about a general who was discussing with his staff about how to take a difficult position. One of his officers suggested a certain course of action. He said, "It will only cost the lives of a few men." The general replied, "Are you willing to be one of the few?"

Jesus was not that kind of a leader. What He demanded that they should face, He too was ready to face. Jesus had a right to call on us to take up a cross, for He Himself first bore one. My friend, if you will follow Christ, you must say no to your natural love of ease and comfort. You must say no to every course of action based on self-seeking and self-will. Say no to the desires that lead you to forbidden ways.

Say yes to the voice and command of Jesus. Remember the words of the Apostle Paul as he said that it is no longer he who lives, but Christ who lives in him. You must no longer live to follow your own will, but to follow the will of Christ. It is in His service that you will find your present freedom.

Dear reader, the cross that the Lord asks us to carry can take us on a difficult and narrow path. We may have to think kind and loving thoughts about someone who has given us a very difficult time and to speak to him with a kind and tender heart. We may have to mention our Master among those who do not wish to be reminded of Him and His promises. I may actually "move among my race and show a glorious morning face" when my heart is sore and hurting, but remember, Jesus is so very near to us as we lift our cross, lay it quietly on our shoulder, and set about with a loving and patient Spirit.

It is at the cross-bearing time that He deepens our peace, increases our courage, gives us extra power to serve others in our distressing hours, and brings our wisdom into full bloom. "You may others from sadness to gladness file, if you carry your cross with a smile!"

Let us recognize the fact that no teacher ever had a higher view of man that Jesus did. No one ever threw such commands at men; no one ever threw such challenges at men; no one ever came to man with such an invitation.

The important thing to Jesus was not so much what man was, but what He could make him. He comes to us with a way of sacrificial love and loyalty and service. Shall we take the way of our own impulses, or shall we take the divine way? Sin is doing what we like, allowing our will to take the place of God's will. It is placing yourself in the middle of the picture. Jesus wants us to focus our eyes upon Him, and sin is deliberately refusing God's invitation. The tragedy at the heart of the parable of the prodigal son is that the son thought that he knew better than the father. Yes, men can see the highest and still refuse it.

Men can be confronted with God's holy command, His perfect truth, and they can refuse it, reject it, remain blind to the truth, and that, my friend, is sin. God is the only cure for sin. Sorry to say, but the plain truth of life is that a man may master his actions, but he cannot master his thoughts and desires. He does need some power outside and beyond himself.

The only cure for sin, the only solution to man's failure to take up his cross, is found in the indwelling power of God. You are not a man, and you do not reach manhood until you can say with the Apostle Paul, "It is no longer I who lives, but Christ who lives within me." Write these words on the tablet of your heart as they come to you from James 1:5: "If any of you lacks wisdom, he should ask God, who gives generously to all, without finding fault, and it will be given to him."

Mark's Gospel calls us to be followers, servants, of Christ. The teachings of Jesus encourage us to reject the worldly way of seeking pleasure, but command us to follow Him and serve others. Following Jesus means that we are called to serve Him and to serve others in His name.

Dear reader, the words written by Mark concerning the cross were well understood in Rome. Death on a cross was a form of execution for dangerous criminals. The criminal was forced to carry the cross to the place of execution. Therefore, Jesus used that cross-bearing image to show how His followers were to be in submission to Him. Jesus was never against our having fun, and He definitely never said that we should seek pain needlessly. He was simply showing them that to carry the cross, to follow Him, is not only difficult, but also spiritually trying at times.

Always keep in mind that we should be willing to lose our lives for Christ, not because our lives are unimportant, but because of what we gain through Christ. He wants us to choose to follow Him rather than to lead a life of sin and self-satisfaction. In other words, may the Lord help us to lose our self-centered determination. You and I both know many worldly types, people who spend their time and energy seeking earthly pleasures. When they focus on possessions, status, or power, etc., they are wasting their time. Whatever you have on earth is temporary. Oh, yes, it may give you pleasure temporarily, but in the final analysis, your life will be hollow and empty.

Let us here and now decide. Shall we follow Christ, or continue in the selfish pursuit of worthless pleasures? I will guarantee you that to follow Jesus will give you an abundantly pleasurable and fruitful life, followed by an eternal life with Him. Let us choose today: we can reject Jesus now and be rejected by Him at the second coming, or we can accept Him now and be accepted by Him when He returns for us. True, rejecting Christ may help us find those so-called worldly pleasures now, but it will result in eternal damnation. Our wisdom comes from His Word.

Almighty God, who through the love of thy Son, Jesus Christ, has given us a great light to dawn upon the darkness. Grant, we pray thee, that in His light we may see light to the end of our days. Bestow upon us, we beseech thee, that most excellent gift of your wisdom, along with your divine love to all men. May the likeness of thy Son encompass our hearts, and surrendering all to Him, may we enjoy everlasting life, eternally with Thee. Amen.

Luke

There are many significant spiritual delights in the reading of Luke's Gospel, but one in particular is stressed throughout his writing: he presents Jesus Christ as the Savior of the whole human race. Throughout his Gospel, he emphasizes how kind and loving Jesus is to those of His day who were despised by society, such as tax collectors, Samaritans, the poor, and the women. I love the way he stresses the importance of prayer in Jesus's life. Before we get into the reading and study of Luke's Gospel, I would ask you: have you repented of your sins, and have you claimed Jesus as your own personal Savior? Do you show the same sort of compassion to others that Jesus showed? Wisdom says, "Take it to the Lord in prayer."

In choosing one passage that summarizes the message of the Gospel of Luke, I give you Jesus's own text and sermon at Nazareth. "The Spirit of the Lord is on me, because He has anointed me to preach good news to the poor. He has sent me to proclaim freedom for the prisoners and recovery of sight for the blind, to release the oppressed, to proclaim the year of the Lord's favor" (Luke 4:18–28). It is up to all of us to tell the world of His words of grace, of the powerful miracles He performed, along with the crucified and risen Savior, who is alive in us today and forever.

Yes, dear reader, Luke has shown in his Gospel with skill and sympathy just how the poor and lonely people of the land welcomed Jesus into their arms. And, even now, through the power given to us by the victorious Savior, we must go out into the world and lift Him up to draw all men to Him. Yes, Jesus was arrested and executed, but death could not destroy Him. He came back to life and ascended into heaven. Let us truly and gratefully accept the forgiveness that Jesus offers to each of us.

Luke was a medical doctor and historian. He skillfully and ever so brilliantly lets us see how the Holy Spirit was sent by God to affirm the Savior's authority and to give the Holy Spirit to His people. By faith, we can have the indwelling Holy Spirit's power and presence to help us to witness and serve Him.

Dear friend, Luke had a reason for listing the many miracles and parables of Jesus. As you must know, only the God-fearing Christian can truly appreciate the love of God. We can readily see the huge distance between a Holy God and a sinful creature such as you and me. Luke shows us the love that fills the space between us and the Father. The gap was closed by the death of the Lord Jesus Christ.

This is well shown in Luke 13:11–13: "And behold, there was woman who had a spirit of infirmity of eighteen years, and was bowed together, and could in no-wise lift up herself. And when Jesus saw her, He called her to Him and said to her, 'Thou art loosed from thine infirmity.' And He laid His hand on her and immediately she was made straight and glorified Him!"

My friend, this miracle actually took place in a synagogue and on the Sabbath. I point this out to you for a good reason. The place where the greatest miracles that are needed today is within the Christian church. Let us all pray that somehow God will take hold of the crooked Christians, like this crooked woman, and make them straight that they might hereafter glorify Him.

True, the world is a very difficult place to live in. It does have immense problems and is in the grip of the enemy, who is very powerful. True, but God has no problem with the world. The Lord Jesus looked into the face of His disciples and said, "Be of good cheer. I have overcome the world!" Yes, we too think the devil is all-powerful, and he is very clever, but the Lord Jesus at the Cross stripped him of his power and defeated him outright. God's problem is not with the world; it is with us. Not with His enemies, but with the people who have been redeemed by His precious blood. By God's grace, Jesus has given us all of the resources of heaven that we might live gloriously for His honor and for

His praise. Yes, to get us to live in His will, to get crooked Christians made straight—that is God's problem.

Dear reader, look at the condition of this woman, her needs, and how it does reflect our needs as well. She was bent double (in Greek, as Luke would tell you, she had a condition known as "neurathenia," a lost connection between the mind and the body). In Romans 7, Paul says, "With my mind I serve the Law of God, but with my flesh, the law of sin." Sounds familiar? It happens to all of us—neurasthenia. In spite of the fact that we claim to be born again and that we claim to have received into our hearts our loving Savior, we are still bent double. We are still earthbound. There is no victory.

But wait, in Romans 8:1–3, it says, "Therefore, there is now no condemnation for those who are in Christ Jesus, because through Christ Jesus the law of the Spirit of life set men free from the law of sin and death, for what the law was powerless to do, in that it was weakened by the sinful nature, God did by sending His own Son in the likeness of sinful man to be a sin offering, and so He condemned sin in sinful man." As we read in Luke 13:12, "When Jesus saw her, He called her forward and said, "Woman, you are set free from your infirmity!" That is wisdom for all of us to observe. In the act of trusting Jesus, she had all of her sins forgiven. For you and for me, "there is no condemnation to them that are in Christ Jesus."

Hallelujah and Amen!

My dear friend, look at how Jesus met this woman's needs. We all have needs in our lives as well. What did Christ do about it? He saw her. He saw her in a way that nobody else ever did, and I assure you, He sees you differently from the way that anybody else ever sees you. He wants to look into your heart as you really are. Will you allow Him to do it? Come right out into the open before Him with an honest confession. I believe you want to open up to Him because you know He has been calling you to Him for a long, long time. Perhaps, that is why you are reading this book at this time. In His mercy, He has seen you, and He is calling you to Him. There is no gradual unbending, no gradual straightening out. He looked into her face and into her heart, and He saw her completely. He saw her need as she lifted that longing heart to Him. Then, He said, "Woman, thou art loosed from thine infirmity."

Behind those words is the authority of an empty Cross and empty tomb and the outpouring of His Holy Spirit to come into your life—all to make you straight. Has God made you straight? Others do not care about our Christianity. They can be indifferent to it because we are broken and earthbound. But if the Holy Ghost fills our life and makes us clean and straight and pure men of God, then others will see us, as they saw this woman—glorifying God! "Thou art loosed from thine infirmity!" The sins are disposed of in the response of your yielding and in your faith. He will smash sin's power, and you will be free. Do you believe that? God Bless you. Your wisdom has made you victorious in Him.

In the Book of Luke, we find words of wisdom coming directly from our Savior. In Mark also, we found Jesus saying, "For who is greater, the one who is at the table, or the one who serves? But I am among you as one who serves." In these words, our Master is standing opposed to those selfish, self-centered ones who compel others to serve them. His wisdom is telling us that true greatness is in those who yield themselves up entirely to serve others. Yes, the desire to be served in our society today is appalling to Him. He is letting us know that service given, not gained, is the sign of true greatness, and our greatness in Him is the result of our self-emptying and the yielding of ourselves to serve others.

Dear friend, God's greatness is in the depth and grace of His amazing stoop to our humanity and to the death on the Cross. He reigns in our lives because He laid His glory aside to serve. I ask you, shouldn't you and I then seek greatness in Him by eagerly serving others? Let us serve in fellowship with Jesus.

I am convinced that by our dying to self, the crucifying of pride, we find the path to heavenly joy. Wisdom tells us that if we want power, we have to be assertive. If we want joy, we have to learn to be submissive. And, dear friend, it is only when we die to self that we can fully love one another. I ask you, how can we ever hope to love others when self is screaming for constant care? We must either live for self or crucify it. Let us crucify self to increase the level of love around us, for only when we die to self can we fully love one another.

Finally, dear reader, when Jesus was asked to name the great commandments in the scriptures, He immediately offered these magnificent words of wisdom: "Love the Lord your God with all your heart and with all your Soul and with all your mind...Love your neighbor as yourself." These three aspects of love are the most effective weapon against the destructive power of the big ego, self-centeredness, and appalling selfishness so prevalent in the world today. Genuine love is a gift we give to others. It is a decision we make on a daily basis that shows that someone is special and valuable to us. Let us pray for a loving heart. "The greatest prayer anyone can pray is, "Create in me a pure heart, O God, and renew a steadfast spirit within me." Let us write these words of wisdom on the tablets of our hearts.

In our memories, we have often faced the yearning of our Lord Jesus, His searching look of wounded love. Even now, Father, we reach into our back-sliding hearts on many occasions, and with tears of sorrow. We thank you, Father, that your grace has always been sufficient, that your forgiveness has renewed our strength. The memories of those early years are still shining brightly, but in our Christ-loving hearts, we have found victory! Through your Holy Spirit, the Wisdom has conquered all! Amen.

John

In order to introduce you to the Gospel of John, I will use a passage from Isaiah 9:2–6: "Before those people lived in darkness but now they have seen a Great Light. They lived in a dark land, but a Light has shined on them. A child has been born to us. God has given a Son to us. He will be responsible for leading the people, His name will be Wonderful Counselor, Powerful God, Father Who Lives Forever, Prince of Peace."

Dear friend, John wants you to know that by submitting yourself to Christ, by absorbing yourself in His teaching, by living out the events in your life with Him, including all of the emotions and passions with their powerhouse of love and devotion to all, and by living with and in Him, we can be reborn to become new men and women in a new world. Christ does show us what life really is and what our true destiny is. We escape from darkness and live in His Light.

These are the truths that John brings to us in his Gospel. John's Gospel is more than "the life of Christ." It is a powerful statement, demonstrating that Jesus was, and is, the very heaven-sent of God and the only source of eternal life. Yes, John's stated purpose for writing this Gospel was to show that Jesus was the Son of God. John clearly and systematically presented the evidence for Jesus's claims. When evidence is presented in a courtroom, those who hear it must make a choice. You too must choose—is Jesus the Son of God, or not? You are the jury. You must decide. Read John's Gospel and believe.

John tells exactly who Jesus was in the very first words of the Gospel. "In the beginning was the Word, and the Word was with God, and the Word was God. He was with God in the beginning." In every chapter, John shows us that Jesus was God in human form. The greatest sign of Jesus's divinity is in the resurrection, and John provides a moving eyewitness account of finding the empty tomb. Then, he describes the after resurrection appearances of Jesus. On the third day after He died, Jesus rose from the dead. This was verified by His disciples and by many other eyewitnesses.

Beloved reader, take great joy in knowing that the same power that raised Christ to life can give you the ability to follow Christ in all of the days of your life. We can all be changed as the disciples were and realize that one day we will be raised to be with Christ forever.

Yes, it is absolutely true—wisdom does come in many forms and down many avenues of life, but in the Gospel of John, true wisdom is found in His Word. John 1:14 says,

"The Word became flesh, and made His dwelling among us. We have seen His glory, the glory of the one and only, who came from the Father, full of grace and truth." This description, given by John, shows very clearly that he is speaking of Jesus. Jesus was a human being that John knew and loved deeply, and yet, at the same time, He was the creator of the universe, the Holy Father of us all.

John, the devoted follower of Christ, has given us a personal and powerful look at Jesus Christ, the eternal Son of God. As you read here and contemplate the messages before you, meditate upon them and commit yourself to believe and to follow Him. Through the power of His indwelling Holy Spirit, His wisdom will guide you, protect you, and lead you into His eternal love. Dear reader, remember the occasion on which these words of Christ were spoken and recorded for us in John 15:1–5: "I am the true vine and my Father is the gardener. He cuts off every branch in me that bears no fruit, while every branch that does bear fruit He prunes so that it will bear even more fruitful. You are already clean because of the word I have spoken to you. Remain in me, and I will remain in you. No branch can bear fruit by itself; it must remain in the vine. Neither can you bear fruit unless you remain in me."

Our Lord had gathered His twelve apostles into the upper room. He started the evening's proceedings by washing their feet. He instituted the Last Supper. He showed the one who was to betray Him by passing the sop to Judas.

Then, after Judas had gone out, He began to talk to the remaining eleven. He told them that He would soon be leaving them. That was something they simply could not understand, and distress and sorrow were written on their faces. He then proceeded to emphasize that they would not be left alone or comfortless—He was coming to them. Remember, He told them where He was going and that He would prepare a place for them. He told them of the gift of the Holy Spirit that would come into their hearts and be His "other self" to dwell within them.

Then, there came a moment when our Lord said, "Arise, and let us go hence." After having the Passover prayer and singing the Passover hymns, they went out into the darkness and into the silent streets of the city. Our Lord led them on the way to the Mount of Olives and the Garden of Gethsemane. As they moved through the temple courtyard and with the moon shining upon the dome of the temple, they could see the great golden vine circling the dome of the temple as a symbol of the life of Israel entwined about the sanctuary of God. As they passed by, it seemed that the Lord paused for a moment and pointed to that vine, saying, "I am the true vine…"

What was the Lord telling them? Remember, the vine was a symbol of Israel, God's chosen people.

The prophet Isaiah long before had written, "My well beloved hath a vineyard in a very fruitful hill; and he fenced it, and gathered out the stones thereof, and planted it with the very choicest vine, and built a tower in the midst of it, and also made a wine press therein; and he looked that it should bring forth grapes, and it brought forth wild grapes."

Dear reader, that is why God had created this people of Israel. He had chosen them to be His witnesses to the world, chosen them to be the people in whom His glory could be shown to the nations around them and to show them His holiness, His justice, His mercy, His redeeming purpose for you and me. Israel was chosen to carry the message of His Holy Spirit and His salvation to the ends of the earth.

However, she failed. She failed in her ministry and in carrying the message to the world. You see what happened—she turned in upon herself. I must point this out because this is a common point of failure, not only in nations, but also in human beings such as you and I. Instead of going out into the world in God's name, instead of revealing the message of His glory, His majesty, His holiness, we turn to ourselves. We become selfish and self-seeking and filled with corruption of all types. And by our selfishness and our sins, we lose our understanding of God's will for us. We lose the enjoyment of the indwelling presence of the Holy Spirit. By pointing to the symbol of the vine, Jesus is saying to you and to me: "I am the true vine—all that you have failed to be and all that others have failed to find in you, you will find in me. The life and the love of God, the Word and the will of God, the justice and the mercy of God, the

Spirit and the presence of God—all that should have been seen in you, you can see in me. I am the true vine."

Dear reader, this is the true message of the Gospel—that which we cannot find anywhere else, we can find in the Lord Jesus. Yes, my friend, God has given us blessings to enjoy, and you will find all of the blessings of enjoyment in the person and in the love of His dear Son, our Lord and Savior Jesus Christ.

My wife and I toured Italy a few years ago, and we saw vineyards everywhere. Flowers were in full bloom. Believe me, I can't remember what the flower of a vine looks like. Who thinks about the flower anyway? Isn't it that way with Christ as well? In Him, there is no artificial pretense of influence or beauty or power. He showed only the depth of His meekness, His humility, His simplicity, and the purity of His patience.

Think of those rich, heavy clusters of fully ripe grapes, huge bunches hanging everywhere. The flower is small, but the fruit is abundant. It is the grapes that give the vine its distinctive quality, and yet, the treasure of the grapes is torn down. Why is that? Yes, this year's grapes are for others to enjoy. The vine is cut back in order to ensure a rich growth and more fruit in the year to come. Jesus says we are the branches, and the branches are to bear His fruit. I ask you, my friend, what is this fruit?

The fruit of the life of our Lord Jesus Christ in His people—you and me—is fruit of the Christ-like character.

"The fruit of the Spirit is love, joy, peace, long-suffering, gentleness, goodness, meekness, patience, self-control"—this is the fruit of His people as shown by the life of Jesus Christ. These are shown in the lives of those who live for others. They can only be expressed in relation to others. I ask you, how can love be seen in you unless you love others? And goodness, gentleness, meekness, self-control, all of these are seen only in relation to those about you; the fruit is for others to enjoy.

So often we Christians think of our own enjoyment and satisfaction are all right, but it is much better to pray, "O Lord, the hearts of so many people around me are hurting and suffering in so many ways, pour out your blessings through me that I may satisfy them." This is the very heart and center of the Christian message. Why did Christ die? Look at it in this light, my friend: this is a tearing down of the grapes of the heavenly vine so that others could share His eternal life. He died to save sinners. He died to atone for our sins. He laid down His life, which was perfect, the giving of the only life ever lived here on earth that brought down on itself the approval of the Father and upon whom the Holy Spirit came to make us His abiding home. That life was cut down so that the human experiences of our hearts might find eternal joy.

You, my dear Christian friend, are rooted in Christ, and, therefore, you are a branch of the vine. It is the life of Christ that you are here to express to others. This is the sacrificial heritage you have as a Christian. You now live in Christ as a branch of the heavenly vine, and this glorious fruit can be borne in your life

Have you accepted God's sacrificial purpose for your life? Have you realized that God saved you in order that you might live no longer for yourself, but in and for Him? Until now, your life, like Israel, has been turned in upon yourself. You have been taken up with your own concerns, and your own interests have preoccupied you. You have lived for yourself. But Jesus says that once you have learned to abide in Him and be filled with the Holy Spirit, He will turn you inside out, and from you will flow rivers of living water. You see, it is for others that you live; you give God's resources to others for their comfort and for their salvation.

Dear reader, think—life is not only for me, but also for others. And remember, yes, we are the branches, but there is one who loves the vine—the Husbandman. The vine is His Son, and in His son are His people, His children, you and me. The vine-dresser is the Father. He loves the vine so dearly that He holds in His hands a pruning knife. The Father has such a love for this vine and its branches that have been fruitful, and He cuts it back. Why? Because He wants that branch to be more fruitful.

To illustrate the pruning process, I'll give you a personal example. I have many rose bushes. I say, "I love my rose bushes so much that I'll leave it alone, I'll let it grow." It will grow through the years, and every year it will grow wilder and wilder, and the quality of the roses will decrease until at last they're in the wilderness. No, if you love your rose bush, you must prune it. The Father loves you so much that He will surely prune you. But are you living as a branch of that vine?

Yes, my friend, you are a branch, but have you accepted wholeheartedly your calling? Have you taken up the sacrificial life? Have you yielded yourself wholly to Christ? Are you living as fully in the vine? As the Lord said, "You must go on growing in me, and I will grow in you. It is the man who shares my life and whose life I, who proves fruitful, share.

Dear friend, you must look to Christ as the source and the strength of your life. You must trust Him to fill you with the Holy Spirit and to perfect in you the kind of character that will express His loveliness and His love and His will. As you increase your love for Him by cultivating this deep, abiding fellowship with Him, you will find yourself growing in grace and in fruit bearing. His Word and His Spirit will become the inspiration of your life.

God Is Awake

When the disasters, the sorrows, came into my life,
And I felt devastated, torn all apart,
I faced the challenges, stood up to the strife—
Took courage—approached them with heart.

Those lesser problems that disrupted my goal,
Causing discomfort, with some pain and grief,
Were confronted with patience and self-control,
Until I soon found my sweet relief.

When the long hard day has finally ended,
All work was finished, I'd done my best,
Those worrisome cares were all mended,
Forgotten, and quietly laid to rest.

I enjoyed a leisurely evening of reading.
Giving my soul a calm soothing break,
With my hours of repose rapidly receding,
I slept in peace, knowing that my God is awake!

—Russell Young

We demonstrate our love of Christ as we live out our lives by trusting and being obedient to His Holy Word, and this is wisdom in action. Through the wisdom of the indwelling Holy Spirit, we know that Christ glorified God by giving Himself in the work of His redeeming love. Yes, my friend, God's glory is His Holiness, and in God's Holiness is His redeeming love. Jesus not only told of the Father being the righteous one who condemns sin and the loving one who saves everyone who turns from sin, but He obediently gave Himself to be a sacrifice, a servant of love even unto death.

It was by His obedience that Jesus glorified God and gave His life to magnify God's love and His Holiness by

His atoning love for us. By Jesus's life, He showed us how the Father loves and how the Father must condemn sin, and yet, in His love, saves the sinner. Yes, Jesus lived, and He died in order to glorify the Father's holiness and the Father's love and, thereby, gave us the victory over the evil sins of the flesh, and also to bring His light into the hearts of His children. He obeyed the Father.

Let us mark our lives by simple obedience. Wisdom says, "Trust and obey." Let everything be done for the Lord, by His will, and to glorify Him. You and I shall let God's glory shine out in the holiness of our lives. Are you honoring Him in your life?

It has been said that love is anything but a natural virtue. Maybe that is why God has made it the defining characteristic of His people. We must dispose of all signs of selfishness. This will only be found in those who have been transformed into new creatures.

So, dear reader, love is to be our defining characteristic. It will remain after faith is completely settled and after our hopes are completely satisfied. Love will last forever because it is being planted and grown and sown into the hearts of people who will live on into eternity.

John was known as the apostle Christ loved, and love gave him his legacy. He had discovered the secret of Christian living, the glue that binds the different classes of people, and the one item that distinguishes the church in the world. Love never fails. John 3: 23 says, "And this is His command: To believe in the name of the Son, Jesus Christ, and to love one another as He commanded us."

Wisdom tells us that love draws us about as close to the heart of God as you can get. My friend, you will probably face a situation today that will give you an opportunity to demonstrate that love and let you find out for yourself. Don't you agree that one's love for God is equal to the love one has for the person he loves best?

The True Vine

Jesus said, "I am the true vine,"
Unto Him I shall faithfully cling,
Earthly possessions are no longer mine,
I've surrendered them all to the King.
He is my anchor and my guiding light,
His anointment has made me whole.
My life is secure, my future is bright,
Eternity abides in my soul.
I am a true branch of the living vine,
Producing the fruit for His precious fold,
Showing the world how His love divine,
Will purify their hearts of gold.
Witnessing to others in so many ways,
With compassion filling my heart,
Obeying His Word, giving Him all the praise,
Always lifting Him up from the start.
Through the Holy Spirit abiding within,
And with self crucified, I am free
To deliver the message received from Him,

Loving others as He has loved me.
Humbly devoted to all who come near,
And with nourishment from Him up above,
This faithful branch proceeds without fear,
Witnessing to the true vine of love.

—Russell Young

Peter

The one major fact that we must always keep in mind as we read the letters from the Apostle Peter is this: he was writing to a group of Christians who had been suffering for their faith. Peter is reminding the people of how much Jesus suffered. He inspires them with hope for the future and shows them how to grow in their faith. False teachers are troubling the church and disturbing some by their heresy, immorality, and greed. Peter wants Christians to grow in the knowledge of the truth of God's Word in order to gain wisdom.

Dear friend, as you read these pages, I would encourage you to decide to do your best to live a holy life as you look forward to the return of Jesus and to the reward He promises to give His followers. Remember, God will eventually win the battle against false teachings. Let us all promise the Lord that we will study to increase our knowledge of His Holy Word.

Let us read from the book of Matthew 5:14–15: "You are the light of the world. A city on a hill cannot be hidden. Neither do people light a lamp and put it under a bowl. Instead they put it on its stand, and it gives light to everyone in the house." All of us have accepted Christ as our Lord and Savior, and we have "put on Christ" as our new identity. Now, we are bound to live holy lives, and our actions should bear witness to our growth in Him. That may well be why the world around us today is in darkness. Since we have been called by God to live a holy life, and since it is beyond our natural ability to achieve it, then it follows that God Himself must give us the light, the strength, and the courage to fulfill the task He requests of us. He will definitely give us the grace we need. If we do not achieve holiness, it is because we do not turn to Him for His gift of grace.

Dear reader, always keep in mind that no darkness, no matter how large or permanent in appearance, can stop the light of God's power. Just a single stroke of white paint on a canvas can completely change the mood of a picture, and, in the same way, a single ray of divine light will change the blackest, most hopeless life into one of promise, potential, and ultimate glory.

We should not worry that in our country today it may seem that Christians are in a minority. In Peter's day, those who were truly spiritual were in a minority. I do see a parallel of his time in our lives today, and I see things steadily getting worse. But God has His remnant today, just as

He did then. You and I, as committed followers of Christ, are part of that remnant. Through us, God will change the world.

Hallelujah!

Think of how marvelous it is to be able to say that we are sons of God, brothers of Christ, temples of the Holy Spirit, and blesses with His Wisdom in this world!

Today we live in times of great confusion, strife, and uncertainty. The balance of power appears to be shifting away from us, and the newspapers, along with television, make us wonder what will happen next. I often wonder what the next few years are going to hold for our children and grandchildren. However, I do know this: the Lord is Lord, and He is sovereign. He rules over all. He is high and exalted. He is holy and supreme. All of our problems pale in the light of His power.

Yes, my friend, the leaders of the world can strut around on the world's stage, but they are not gods—they are just creatures whom the creator can readily put to shame. Lift up your eyes and your heart to God. Keep Him on His throne in your life, and He will continue reign in holiness.

As I mentioned earlier, Peter is writing to people who have been suffering for their beliefs. We have not had the suffering in America that others throughout the world are seeing. I toured China recently and saw firsthand how distressed and frightened those lovely people are when we mention Christianity to them publicly. It is true in many countries of the world today—Christians still suffer for what they believe in. We should expect it; we do not have to be afraid of it. Knowing that we will live eternally with Christ should give us confidence, patience, and hope to stand firm when nonbelievers persecute us. In spite of all things, Christ is our foundation. We must remain devoted, loyal, and faithful to Him and stand firm under all circumstances.

Look at it in this light: we are accountable to God. Let Him be the judge of others and their behavior. We must not hate those who attack our beliefs. After all, we must accept the fact that we will be held responsible for how we conduct ourselves under all conditions. Let us pray for God's help and strive for self-discipline and submission. He will judge everyone with His perfect justice. We too will face God. He will punish those who persecute, and those who love Him will be rewarded with eternal life in His presence.

In 1 Peter 3:9–12, we find Peter quoting from Psalm 34:12–16: "A person must do these things to enjoy life, and have many happy days. He must not say evil things, and he must not tell lies. He must stop doing evil, and do good. He must look for peace, and work for it. The Lord sees the good that people do, and He listens to their prayers. But the Lord is against those who do evil." Peter is telling us that if we open up our lives to Christ, He will come in, speaking peace, just as He did to His disciples after His resurrection, saying, 'Peace be unto you!'"

My dear friend, Christ comes into our lives today to give us His love, His life, and shares with us His peace. We then become a person of peace. We find what it is to know the way to peace with God, peace with others, and peace with ourselves. In our lives, a dramatic change sets in.

Peace, goodwill, good cheer, and serenity replace the bitterness, hostility, belligerence, jealousy, bad temper, quarreling, etc. The peace of God embellishes our lives, and this peace comes only from Christ. This peace indicates the very presence of Jesus Christ in our lives. Is your life full of the peace of Christ? Pray that God will give you a greater love and a closer understanding of His peace, and that it will reach out to everyone in your life.

Again, Peter quotes from Psalm 71:14: "I will always have Hope, and I will praise God more and more." Dear reader, it is quite obvious to all that Christians do have a corner on hope. Why is this so? Because all hope comes from knowing who God is. Without God, there is no hope. It is God who controls the universe and promises to bring us to heaven. Hope points to the future, and that is where our hope is in. God has a purpose for all people, and He will bring it to an end when He returns as He has promised. As for you and me, our hope lies in our Christian growth here on earth. We hope that we are doing what God wants us to be doing in our lives today. And, yes, we hope for the new heaven and the new earth that God has promised to us. We hope for Christ's second coming, an eternal life, and in our resurrection. We hope that this world is not all there is.

The beautiful part about our hope is that it is supported by the fact that it will happen because our hope is in God, not in ourselves. Proverbs 2:6 says, "Only the Lord gives wisdom: He gives knowledge and understanding." Proverbs 1:1, 3, 7 also tells us: "These are the wise words of Solomon, son of David, king of Israel. They will teach you how to be wise and self-controlled and will teach you to do what is honest, and fair, ad right. Knowledge begins with respect for the Lord, but fools hate wisdom and self-control."

Dear reader, keep in mind that if we are to enjoy His peace, His love, and our hope, we must make every effort to increase our faith, knowledge, self-control, steadfast-ness, and brotherly love. Prayer and Bible study are vital in adding to our faith. God reveals Himself to us in the scriptures, and through our prayers we can go directly to Him with our supplications. God wants us to reach a place of maturity where we can spiritually feed ourselves and be able to stand strong against any and all evils that we may have to face.

Peace of Mind

As our daily quest for peace continues,
Seeking serenity at all times,
We are compelled to ask the question,
"Is peace attainable with our minds?"

Can we develop a habit of thinking
That will overcome failure no matter what?
Can we face danger hour after hour,
The embarrassments or the cares we've got?
Yes…yes, the marvel of being a Christian,
When you strongly and faithfully believe it—
The gift of heavenly peace from Christ
Comes to every soul that will receive it!

—Russell Young

Peter writes a second letter because false teachers are giving the church a hard time and upsetting the faith with their immoralities and their greed. Peter wants Christians to grow in the knowledge of the Truth of God's Word. Remember: wisdom is derived from God's Holy Word. God will eventually win the battle against false teaching. Let each of us promise the Lord that we will study to increase our knowledge of the scriptures.

Simon Peter, a servant and apostle of Jesus Christ. To those who through the righteousness of our God and Savior Jesus Christ have received a faith as precious as ours: grace and peace be yours in abundance through the knowledge of God and of Jesus our Lord. His divine power has given us everything we need for life and godliness through our knowledge of Him who called us by His own glory and godliness. Through these He has given us His very great and precious promises so that through them you may participate in His divine nature and escape the corruption in the world caused by evil desires. For this very reason, make every effort to add to your faith goodness, and to goodness, knowledge, and to knowledge, self-control, and to self-control, perseverance, godliness, and to godliness, brotherly kindness, and to brotherly kindness, love. For if you possess these qualities in increasing measure, they will keep you from being ineffective and unproductive in your knowledge of our Lord Jesus Christ.

Dear reader, keep in mind that Simon Peter, in this letter, is addressing a tricky situation. These people were claiming that they were saved, justified, and forgiven, but you couldn't see it in the way they were living. They talked wonderfully about God, but they lived a life in slavery to some very bad habits. In other words, instead of their faith being something fine and beautiful and fruitful, it was disgracefully filled with the world's corruption. Sounds familiar? Are you seeing something familiar today? Well, Peter is telling them that real faith is never alone; it always produces a fruit crop in the character of the believer. Peter is saying to all of us that it is no good saying, "I know God," if your life plainly shows that you do not know Him. Those false claims destroy the Christian character.

Dear friend, Peter wants each of us to understand that true faith glorifies God in all things. True faith leads us to be nothing but an instrument of His holy will. He is glorified when we simply become a window through which

God's mercy shines on the world. We must strive to be His witnesses, not to show our holiness, but to place His goodness above our selfish, self-centered ways. He who loves God seeks to glorify God and to become, by God's grace, perfect in love, as the "Heavenly Father is perfect."

Interestingly, in the very first words of 2 Peter 1:1–8, we get a clue to the wonder of Peter's calling to Christ. (Simon is "Simeon" in Greek and Peter is the new Christian name.) This draws you back to the day when Simon met Jesus for the first time. To Simon, the rough and tough but lovable character, Jesus said, "You are Simon, but you will be a man of rock. You will be Peter by the time I have finished with you." Simon Peter passed through a wonderful change from the one to the other once he let Jesus Christ take control, and so have you and I. Wisdom has brought us to Christ.

Dear reader, we do have the same precious faith as the first people of the Christian Gospel. We know that God is fair, and His call goes out the same as ever for the people to put their trust in Jesus This call includes the call to you and to me.

I will admit that I often think of my old spiteful nature, and I am amazed to think that in His righteousness, His call has come to me and drawn out a strong response of faith in Him. Think back, how did His call come to you? In my case—and I am sure you had a similar experience—He attracted me by His glory and His virtue and the powerful manliness of His character. Of course, His promises attracted all of us too.

Yes, dear friend, think on those promises—the promise of His love and His forgiveness. Think of His divine power that gives you the strength that is necessary for life and for godliness to live an upright life in this diabolical world. Yes, thank Him every hour for the privilege of possessing His indwelling Holy Spirit. Think of it, isn't it fantastic to be able to say we are sons of God, brothers of Christ, and that we are temples of the Holy Spirit and born from above, Blessed with His wisdom in the world? All of this comes through His gracious love. It is by the sheer love of God that you have been lifted out of a life of futility and corruption that surround us in this world of lust and selfishness.

All of us were long lost sinners, but by God's mercy and the grace of the Lord Jesus Christ, we have been adopted into His family, not by any effort on our part, but by the sheer love of Almighty God. Thanks be to God. Adore Him, praise Him, worship His almighty name, love Him, and love others as He has loved you.

And now I ask you, what should be our response to God's mercy and grace that has transformed our lives? Let us have another look at Peter's words beginning in verse 5: "For this very reason, make every effort to add to your faith goodness; and to goodness, knowledge…" Yes, we all know that Christ's calling inevitably leads to improvements in the Christian conduct, but obviously the false teachers would never believe this. They will say that once you have faith, no need to worry about your behavior, you're okay. This simply suggests that God is not interested in conduct; however, He is! True, it is only by the grace of God that we can make an effort, but without our additional qualities, we will not gain the power of God's will to transform our lives.

The Christian knows that these qualities are the fruits of the Holy Spirit within us. This ends in the likeness to Christ that is the object of God's saving work. You have to make your contribution to what God is doing. He wants to assist you. You cannot do it alone; you are "weak and He is strong." Add to your faith, and God will add to it too.

My dear Christian friend, please meditate upon this point: many believers want an abundance of God's grace and peace, but they are not willing to put forth the effort to know Him better through Bible study and prayer. Are you enjoying the grace that God gives you freely, such as "the knowledge of God and of Jesus our Lord"? His wisdom is yours when you put forth the effort to attain it.

You and I, as solid Christians, are well aware of the fact that faith must be more than belief in all biblical knowledge. Faith must result in action, growth in Christian character, along with the practice of moral discipline, or it will be weakened and fade away. Let us learn of Peter's faith in action—drawing ever nearer to God, gaining perseverance, obeying God's will, loving others. These actions do not just happen automatically; they require your best efforts. They are not optional, but they must be continually at work in your daily life. Yes, dear reader, God does give us strength, and He does enable us, but He also expects us to learn and to grow in fellowship with Him.

Let us not seek our own glory, dear Christian, but seek to glorify God in all ways. Keep in mind that in order to glorify God, we must be nothing but an instrument in doing all things for Him. We—you and I—must be simply a window through which God's love and benevolence will shine in the world. For this to happen, we must always try to be holy, striving to be virtuous in all things. Now, we are not just striving to be a holy person, not striving just to be holy and virtuous, but making sure that the goodness and the love of God may never be diminished by any selfish act of ours. We who love God seek the glory of God and seek to become, by His grace, perfect in virtue and in love, as "the Heavenly Father is perfect" (Matthew 5:48).

For instance, virtue means goodness in action. A so-called Christian who is semi-moral and tends to go the worldly way is a discredit. Selfishness, dishonesty, greed, etc., are a menace to Christianity. We are to be the window through which others see Christ-likeness and will want to come to Jesus.

Knowledge: Do you know Jesus better today than you did a year ago? Peter wants Christians to remain in the scriptures to add knowledge to their faith—in other words, to help us to bring others to Christ through wisdom found in the Word. Therefore, we should be adding knowledge to our faith daily throughout our entire lives.

Supposing you were asked to explain your faith to someone today—a liberal, a communist, or a particular college professor—have you any way to commend your faith in an intelligent way to them? If not, it is time for you to add to your faith knowledge, and then add to knowledge self-control and self-discipline. Do people see self-control in you? For instance, self-control in the way we talk about other people when they are not present. Are you disciplined with your money? You should spend your money in a way that you would not be ashamed if Christ were standing next to you. Are you disciplined in your prayer life? In your Bible reading? In tithing?

To your self-control, add endurance and patience. As I am writing these words, the TV is on so loud I can hardly concentrate. I could scream at them to turn it off, or I could be calm and endure it. I learned a good deal about endurance when I was on the track team at Heidelberg College. Athletes who are generally experts in physical endurance often talk about "pushing through the pain." You cannot stop running when you are winded or exhausted or have pain in your side; you must keep going, knowing that somehow, at the end of the race, the pain will be worth the prize. So it is in our spiritual lives. When adversities come—and make no mistake, they will come—the person of endurance keeps going. When the relationship seems to be hopelessly bogged down, when the outcome just doesn't seem worth the effort, when God is silent and the future seems dim, we push forward and anticipate the finish line. We hold on. We trust. We endure.

Dear friend, we will discover, perhaps, not immediately, that our Heavenly Father is still there, even though His whispers might not have reached our ears. Our self-control, endurance, and patience will remain in God's glorious presence.

The Wise Fools

To please all the fools,
And to fool all the wise,
I made up puzzles that were easy—
The answers seemed to fall from the skies.

When the questions were all completed,
They each began to mutter,
For the fools and the wise alike
Were flying all aflutter!

The fool feels like he is so wise,
And the wise are always so sure,
Each of them so quick to confess,
Their ways and means they prefer.

However, it is the morally wise
Who shall eventually receive the prize.
The fool shall go down to disgrace;

Yes, all we need do is to look around,
For the answers are so easily found—
But they must flow from God's majestic grace!

—Russell Young

My friend, wouldn't you agree that wisdom tells us that what we are asked to endure is absolutely nothing in comparison to what Jesus endured for us? It is the faith that endures to the end, the faith that is the mark of the man who is saved.

Add to your endurance godliness, a deep and abiding reverence for God, Holy awe that sees God in everything and in everyone that we meet. A godliness that sees God and God's challenge in the sick, the lonely, the depressed, in all of the people that we know. Showing true godliness in everything that we do and in everyone we meet will show up in our character. We won't notice it, but others will. The godly man sees the Lord always before him. Godliness means more or less God-likeness, Christ-likeness—reminding people of Him.

Add brotherly kindness; godliness cannot exist without brotherly affection. The Apostle John said, "If any man says, 'I love God,' and does not love his brother, he is a liar." How warm is your love for your brethren, for other Christians? Brotherly kindness means lifting each other's burdens. It can also mean being careful not to put a stumbling block in anyone's way. If we were to stop and think to ask ourselves,

"Is this kind?" then we might stop doing a lot of things we say and do.

Love, as it should be, is the last one. Love is the crown of Christian growth. As a matter of fact, the very word *love* was coined by Christians. Love is definitely more than *liking*. God did not *like* the world that He sent His only begotten Son, but God *loved* the world. He gave Himself up for something that wasn't very attractive because He was love; He couldn't help it. If we have that loving relationship with God, others will see it in our character, and they will be influenced and filled with desire for that same quality.

Yes, my dear friend, you can love someone into the kingdom of God. God's own love can be sent into others from your heart by the Holy Spirit. You must let it happen. Men will not turn to a God of love; they won't even believe there is a God of love until they see it in us, His followers.

Well, now you know the fruits of the tree of faith. As a great Christian writer once said, "It all begins with faith, and it all ends in love." Make those fruits the foremost part of your daily being. You are a child of God, and, therefore, you must add all seven of those fruits to assist your Christian growth. Do not be an idle, fruitless Christian with nothing to bring to your heavenly King. Your character is the proof of your calling, and our character is the only thing we will carry out of this life with us. Yes, that is correct—it is the only thing you can take with you.

Wisdom tells us that the man who has let Christ plant the tree of faith in his life and given it room to grow has a happy and joyful entrance into the heavenly kingdom. He will not be ashamed to meet the Lord. It says in 2 Peter 3:14–15: "So then, dear friends, since you are looking forward to this (a new heaven and a new earth, the home of righteousness), make every effort to be found spotless, blameless, and at peace with Him. Bear in mind that our Lord's patience means salvation, just as our dear brother Paul also wrote you with the wisdom that God gave him!"

I believe it only fitting—considering the fact that our own great nation, the United States of America, seems to be sliding down the slippery slope to immorality—that we should strive to encourage all to remain strong in keeping the commands that our Lord God has given us. After all, what other nation in the world today is so great as to have their God near them the way our Lord God is near us whenever we pray to Him? And what other nation has such righteousness demonstrated in their heritage as our founding fathers have provided for us? Deuteronomy 4:5–6 says, "See, I have taught you decrees and laws as the Lord my God has commanded me, so that you may follow them in the land you are entering to take possession of it. Observe them carefully, for this will show your wisdom and understanding to the nations, whom will hear about these decrees and say, 'Surely this great nation is a wise and understanding people.'"

Amen and God bless America.

Paul

Love

And now, my dear friends, we come to the final chapter of our journey on the road to God's wisdom. It appears that the good Lord has been with us throughout the writing of this book, and obviously His hand has led us to present the Apostle Paul that he may shine forth with his magnificent, God-endowed, spiritual wisdom.

No person, apart from Christ Himself, shaped the history of Christianity like the Apostle Paul. We have all learned since our early years in the scriptures that Paul's miraculous and personal encounter with Christ changed his life forever. Paul was truly a devout, religious man, but he felt that the Christian faith was damaging Judaism. He, therefore, persecuted Christians unmercifully.

And then it happened—God stepped in and stopped him on the road to Damascus. Paul personally met Christ, and, as a result, his life was never the same. Paul was transformed, and the lives that he touched were changed as they met Christ through him. Dear reader, I met Christ at age fourteen at a Sunday evening worship service. This service was at the United Brethren Church on north Pine Street in St. Marys, Ohio.

I sincerely pray that you have had a similar experience and that you will "let your light shine" and that others will see something of Christ in your life. Help others to know the Good News, that forgiveness and eternal life are gifts of God's grace through faith in Jesus Christ. This good news is available to all who seek a loving relationship with the Heavenly Father through Jesus Christ.

Paul has this to say in Philippians 1:21–24: "For to me to live is Christ and to die is gain. If I am to go on living in the body, this will mean fruitful labor for me. Yet, what shall I choose? I do not know! I am torn between the two: I desire to depart and be with Christ, which is better by far; but it is more necessary for you that I remain in the body." Dear reader, Paul is simply saying to all of us, "If you are not ready to die, then you are not ready to live." Be sure of your eternal destiny, and then you will be equipped to serve others, devoting your life to what really counts. Do you have a purpose for living? Whom can you serve or help?

Let us all work together as Christians, caring for the problems of others as if they were our own problems. We must lay aside selfishness and treat others with respect and with sincerely heartfelt love. Link up with the Apostle Paul and with Jesus, and be a true living example of spiritual humility. Like Christ, we must have a servant's attitude, serving out of love for God and for others.

Mark 10: 45 says, "For even the Son of Man did not come to be served, but to serve, and to give His life as a ransom for many." By studying the many letters that Paul wrote to his fellow Christians, we will find a variety of themes that emphasize the significance of our divine transformation. Each and every piece of Paul's writings draws us closer to God and, at the same time, takes us ever nearer to His righteousness and to our salvation. In Paul's letters, we find these three major themes recurring: love, faith, and God's gift of spiritual wisdom.

Paul speaks to us of love:

> If I speak in the tongues of men and of Angels, but have not love, I am only a resounding gong, or a clanging cymbal. If I have the gift of prophecy, and can fathom all mysteries and all knowledge, and I have a Faith that can move mountains, but have not Love, I am nothing. If I give all I possess to the poor, and surrender my body to the flames, but have not love, I gain nothing. Love is patient, love is kind, it does not envy, it does not boast, it is not proud. It is not rude, it is not self-seeking, it is not easily angered, it needs no record of wrongs. Love does not delight in evil but rejoices with the truth. It always protects, always trusts, always hopes, and

> always perseveres. Love never fails. (1 Corinthians
> 13: 1–8)

And in verse 13: "And now, these three things remain forever: faith, hope, and love, and the greatest of these is love." Yes, dear reader, as we just read, "love never fails." However, in the world in which we live today, we see an absolute obsession with romance, or, more specifically, with sex. We are bombarded on all sides by Hollywood's pornographic presentations referred to as "movies," by obscene lyrics in "hit" songs, and on television, which has never been so openly dominated by sexual misbehavior and obscenities galore.

You have heard that "love makes the world go 'round." Well, love does make the world go 'round, but not that kind of love. Agape love, God's selfless love, sets the world in motion and keeps the stars in place. Our Creator's love is the source and center of our universe. Regardless of what society may try to tell us today, God's love is the foundation for all other loves. We as Christians are called to "love as the Lord loved us"—that is, selflessly and sacrificially. We are to offer ourselves to others as God offered Christ to us.

True love does not seek to control anyone. It gives itself freely as a gift without asking for anything in return. As we are all so very well aware of, almost all of the disciples gave up their lives, as did thousands of martyrs down through the ages, and even yet today, not for the love of a woman or the love of a philosophy or some special principle, but for the love of Jesus Christ who had already sacrificed His life for love.

Dear friend, keep this thought always on your mind: love makes our actions and our "giving" of gifts useful. Although people have different gifts, love is available to everyone. Our world today confuses love and lust. God's kind of love, not like lust, is directed toward others, not inward toward ourselves. It is totally unselfish. I would suggest to you that His kind of love is only possible if God helps us to obstruct our own desires and tendencies so that we can love unselfishly and expect nothing in return. In this type of love, we become more Christ-like and the more love we will show to others.

For example, my mother and fathers married life could be likened unto a "stage," on which real love, the love that Paul referred to as the greatest virtue, was openly demonstrated. I still remember thinking, *Lord, please help me to develop such a loving relationship as I am seeing in them.* They had a love that enabled them to endure difficulties with patience and enjoy the good times with exuberant pleasure, and they gave richly of themselves with grace and humility. When all of these virtues are present, not only are they blessed in their marriage, but those lucky enough to observe such a marriage will refuse to settle for less.

Dear reader, what examples of Christian love have you experienced and enjoyed? What did those experiences teach you about love? Have you practiced in your life the love that Jesus has demonstrated in His? The disciples learned the true love from Jesus Himself. He cared about their families, their homes, their problems. He took time to teach them and demonstrated His love in all ways. He forgave them, even when they didn't deserve it. He humbled Himself to them by washing their feet, and He died on Calvary's Cross that they might live with Him forever. And so it is with us if we are to love our brothers and sisters as Jesus commanded. We must show the kind of love our Master has shown us.

Finally, dear reader, the glorious declaration by Jesus, as recorded by Paul, that "love never fails" must go directly from our minds and hearts to our souls. It shows us just exactly that what we have always thought love was is incorrect. It is proof that in God we are absolutely secure. His "Love never fails" gives us eternal strength. When we complete the statement that "God so loved the world (that is, He loved the world *so* much) that He gave His only begotten Son," that my friend is the love that never fails. That love makes our love seem like a false claim. We have so much selfishness within us. So often we love others, but only because they love us. True love, God's love, the love He sends to our souls, comes to us in spite of our unworthiness. That kind of love inspires us to want to serve. It is sacrificial. The more we consider it, the more we feel that we have come up short and helpless. The only way we can love as He loves is if God Himself has possessed and mastered us.

Yes, dear reader, "His love has no limit." Your faith is in God's power, not in human wisdom. God's wisdom does not come from the world or from the rulers of this world who are losing their power. God planned His wisdom for our glory. We received our wisdom from God, not from the world. We received our wisdom from the Spirit of God, and the Spirit is from God so that we can know all things that God has given us.

Men are always seeking greater wisdom, but they usually bypass the ultimate source of wisdom. The scriptures in Proverbs 9:10 tell us, "The fear of the Lord is the beginning of Wisdom, and the knowledge of the Holy One is understanding." It is very true, but man ignores it. Paul says in Romans 1:21–22, "For even though they knew God, they did not honor Him as God, or give thanks; but they became futile in their speculations, and their foolish heart was darkened. Professing to be wise, they became fools."

Dear friend, since God's wisdom resides in His Word, we must maintain a regular time for reading and studying the scriptures. This means delving into the ultimate source of wisdom. I ask you, does God need educated and wise teachers to deliver His message? Are you willing to be that kind of person? Job 28:28 says, "Then He, God, said to humans, 'The fear of the Lord is wisdom to stay away from evil is understanding'" The Apostle Paul placed a high priority on being obedient to Christ and on striving for unity, humility, and Christ's love in the church. Let us all decide to seek the Lord's will in everything we do and to work hard to be humble, to love others, and to become one in spirit with our fellow believers, showing His wisdom in our lives.

The second theme of Paul's writing, and, perhaps, the most prolific part, is centered on the subject of salvation by faith alone. There are twenty-seven books in the New Testament, over half of them were written by one man—the Apostle Paul. Without his letters, we would be almost in total darkness concerning the truth of the church as the Body of Christ and its future. His message was new, received from heaven as a new revelation of divine truth. The heart of this message was the "grace of God" available to all of us and is entirely separate from the "works of the Law," which had been previously limited to the nation of Israel.

Dear reader, the message for us today is: "Believe in the Lord Jesus Christ, and thou shalt be saved." Yes, the sinner is saved by grace without the deeds of the Law. The believers, you and I, are kept by the grace of God without the deeds of the Law. Romans 10:4 tells us, "For Christ is the end of the law…to everyone that believes."

Going Home

Life, like a damaged ship in disaster,
Strenuously struggling to make its way,
Continually cries out to its divine Master,
For help in the days of dread and dismay.

Sailing alone through darkness and fearing,
Wildly tossed like a wind-blown feather,
This floating sphere sustains the steering,
To navigate our way to the shore forever.

Battered by the storms of sorrow and pain,
We seek shelter from these earthly infirmities,
Praying for that day when we shall attain,
His sweet celestial sea of eternity.

—Russell Young

Yes, dear friend, we are free from the Law of commandments, but we are not lawless because we are under a different law—the law of love and devotion. Paul spells it out in Romans 7:4: "You are now dead to the Law by the body of Christ; that you should be married to another, even to Him who is raised from the dead." Life takes the place of death. Love takes the place of the Law. Think of this: where there is absolute love, you need no law. Love goes beyond the demands of the law. This is easily comprehended when we see in a home where love reigns, and each person lives for the other.

How much law do you have there? Do I lay down laws for my wife? No! Because she loves me. She is under the law of love. She works through love. We need no time clock, no laws or rules for wages, or hours. This, my friend, is the service that God desires of us: our love and devotion.

Faith

The service that God expects is the service of love and devotion, our gratitude for His having saved us by grace, and for having delivered us from the curse of the Law. What the Law could not do, the Lord Jesus did do. This is like looking in a mirror and seeing a dirty face, which the mirror cannot cleanse, so we turn to Him who alone by His precious blood has redeemed us and washed our sins away.

> As dedicated messengers of His precious Word,
> Marching steadily forward to our saintly goal,
> We've vowed that all of His children will have heard,
> And that Christ shall dwell within their soul!
>
> —Russell Young

Paul's divine wisdom leaps into your heart and soul as you read in Romans 3: 28: "For we maintain that a man is justified by faith, apart from observing the Law." We do not receive life and salvation because of anything we've done. In fact, the only reason we receive life and salvation is because of God's grace through Christ. There is no other way!

All of us have a difficult time trying to comprehend the depth and attainability of the faith. Even the Apostle Paul admitted that he had not reached this goal. Matthew 5:6 says, "Blessed are those who thirst and hunger forrighteousness, for they will be saved." We must look at it in a positive way—if we are called by God to be holy beyond our natural ability to achieve (and it definitely is), then it follows that God Himself must give us the light, the strength, and the courage to fulfill the task He requires of us. He will definitely give us the grace we need. If we do not reach the goal, it is no one's fault but our own. After all, He has made the gift of His grace available to each of us.

Paul said of Abraham in Galatians 3:6: "Consider Abraham: He believed God, and it was credited to him as righteousness." Paul is simply letting us know that faith in God is the highest worship, the greatest allegiance, the ultimate obedience, and the most pleasing sacrifice. Giving God honor is to believe in Him, knowing He is truthful, wise, righteous, merciful, and all-powerful. He is our Creator and Giver of all things. Faith makes God real to us and in us.

Dear reader, when we honor God in this way, we are showing Him the highest justice, the most pleasing sacrifice, the best worship, and the greatest wisdom possible. God wants you to tell Him your troubles. Do not keep them to yourself. Do not struggle with them alone and torture yourself; it will only multiply your troubles. He knows you are too weak to overcome them by yourself. Grow strong in Him, and then He will be the one who receives the glory. People who are not struggling do not know what faith is all about. It is through the difficult experiences that we emerge as true Christians by our strong faith and God's holy grace.

Dear reader, when we are faced with disasters, when things seem so dark that we even doubt that we are part of the church or pleasing to God, we must learn to reach for the Bible. God considers our reason, our morality, our strength to be weakness and darkness. We must never let those who have fallen from faith lead us astray. Yes, just as we read in 2 Peter 1:19: "And we have the Word of the prophets made more certain, and you will do well to pay attention to it, as to a light shining in a dark place, until the day dawns and the morning rises in your hearts." I ask you, my friend, how is it with your life? Do you have a personal relationship with Jesus Christ? Have you surrendered control of your life to Jesus? Have you made Him Lord of your life?

Paul has these words in Romans 10:8–9: "The Word is near you, it is in your mouth, and in your heart. That is the word of faith we are proclaiming: that if you confess with your mouth Jesus is Lord, and believe in your heart that God raised Him from the dead, you will be saved." Believe and you will be saved. Faith answers all questions. Whenever someone asked Christ about what would be expected of Him as a follower, He always tested their willingness to surrender everything for God's sake. Without that attitude, we cannot even be trusted with material riches because we would waste them on our own indulgences andlusts.

Paul again said in 1 Timothy 6:10: "For the love of money is the root of all kinds of evil. Some people, eager for

money, have wandered from the faith and pierced themselves with many griefs." Yes, it is true that no matter what
you have read in the scriptures, faith is what you are seeking. Faith is not just believing what you've just read. Faith
is not separate from God's grace. In fact, the right kind of
faith flows from God's grace, and, really, what God's Word
demands is this: believe that Christ was born for you. His
birth is yours, and it took place for your benefit. Everything
He did and suffered was for us. "I bring you good news of
great joy that will be for all people. Today in the town of
David, a Savior has been born for you!" For you. With faith,
this joy is for everyone.

Finally, my friend, faith does change people. Their eyes,
ears, and hearts feel something completely different from
what everyone else sensed.

Faith is living and powerful. It is like water that has
been heated. After heating, the water is different. It is still
water, but it is warm. This same thing happens when the
Holy Spirit gives us faith. Faith transforms the mind and
attitudes. It creates an entirely new person. Paul comes
to us from Hebrews 11:9: "By faith (Abraham) made his
home in the Promised Land like a stranger in a foreign
country; he lived in tents, as did Israel and Jacob, who were
heirs with him of the same Promise."

Let us always remember: faith is active, profound, and
powerful. If we are to describe faith correctly, we would say
it is a process, not a result. In other words, my friend, faith

changes the heart and the mind. Admittedly, faith is not as common among people as are the five senses. Considering the number of people in the world, there are relatively few believers. Most people concern themselves with what they can see, touch, and manipulate, rather than listening to God's Holy Word. We have learned from the Apostle Paul that life, grace, and salvation come to us by faith alone, and not by good works. They become ours by eating and drinking the body and the blood of Jesus Christ. Live in the wisdom of the Word.

> Now before you I come humbly,
> My last chance, my only hope,
> Through your love and your conviction,
> I, with steadfast courage, cope,
> Once again to be truly faithful,
> Rejoicing, exulting in a brand new start,
> Mercifully restored and then set free—
> Your loving grace will heal my heart!

—Russell Young

The Holy Spirit

The first emblem under which we see the Holy Spirit in the New Testament is the dove descending upon the head of Jesus at His baptism by the river Jordan. Incidentally, the very first emblem of the Holy Spirit presented in the Old Testament is also a dove.

In Genesis 1, we read, "The earth was without form and void, and darkness *brooded* over the face of the deep, and the Spirit of God *brooded* upon the face of the waters." This, dear reader, is the figure of the mother dove brooding over her nest and protecting her young. Think about this situation: the mother dove of eternal love and peace began at this point to build her nest, and she remained there until that form of evolving material had become a bright and joyful world, a marvelous paradise, with a happy family accepting its pure and heavenly happiness and hope.

And now, some two thousand years later, the world is submerged beneath that awful flood, and all but eight human beings were swept away. Genesis 8:6–12 says:

> And it came to pass, at the end of forty years, that Noah opened the window of the ark which he had made, and he sent forth a raven, which went forth to and fro until the waters were dried up from the earth. Also, he sent forth a dove from him to see if the waters were abated from off the face of the ground, but the dove found no rest for the sole of her foot, and she returned to him into the ark, for the waters were on the whole face of the earth: Then he put forth his hand, and took her in, and pushed her into the ark. And he stayed yet another seven days, and sent forth the dove out of the ark: And the dove came unto him in the evening, and, lo, in her mouth was an olive leaf, plucked off: So Noah knew that the waters were abated from off the earth. And

> he stayed yet another seven days, and sent forth the
> dove, which returned not again unto him anymore.

Let us explore the significance of these events.

First, the dove found no place to rest in the debris. Here we see that the Holy Spirit visited this sinful world but, with no place to abide, went back to God. Then, with the olive leaf in her mouth, we see judgment passed and peace returning. This exemplifies the life and the resurrection of Jesus Christ, reclaiming the sinful world.

Finally, the dove goes forth and returns no more. Thus, it builds its nest in the habitations of men. This final event represents the blessed Holy Spirit's work in our lives today. Yes, dear reader, Jesus has sent the (dove) Holy Spirit forth, and His residence is no longer in Heaven, but is in the heart of every believer and in the heart of the church. This earth is now His home, and here, among sinful, suffering men, that same dove is building her nest and rearing her brood for Heaven's realm and will one day sing and soar in the light of God.

John 16:5–15 tells us that as for the work of the Holy Spirit, Jesus says:

> Now I am going to Him who sent me, yet none of
> you ask me, 'Where are you going?' Because I have
> said these things, you are filled with grief. But I tell
> you the truth: It is for your good that I am going
> away. Unless I go away, the Counselor (Holy Spirit)
> will not come to you; but if I go, I will send Him to

you. When He comes, He will convict the world of guilt in regard to sin and righteousness, and judgment: In regard to sin, because men do not believe in me, in regard to righteousness, because I am going to the Father where you can see me no longer; and in regard to judgment, because the prince of the world now stands condemned. I have much more to say to you, more than you can bear. But when He, the Spirit of Truth, comes, He will guide you into all truth. He will not speak on His own; He will speak only what He hears; and He will tell you what is yet to come. He will bring glory to me by taking from me what is mine and making it known to you. All that belongs to the Father is mine. That is why I said the Spirit will take from me what is mine and make it known to you.

Dear reader, I ask you to etch these words deeply into the recesses of your heart. The Dove—the Holy Spirit—is an emblem of purity. He cannot dwell in an unclean heart or in the sinful mind. "Harmless as a dove" is Christ's description of that lovely emblem. The Holy Spirit also represents the Counselor—gentle, tender, and full of patience and love. The heart in which the Holy Spirit abides will always show gentleness, meekness, and forbearance. Yes, "the fruit of the Spirit is gentleness and meekness." And, perhaps, most significantly, the Holy Spirit is the spirit of love. The very life of this Divine Comforter is to exemplify the love of God in our hearts. Wherever He is, you will recognize

His unselfishness, loving helpfulness, and kindness. The "fruit of the Spirit is love!" He wants us to love Him and to receive His tender love for each of us. Begin today to live in the wisdom of the Holy Spirit.

As I have said, the Apostle Paul's rebirth took place on the road to Damascus, but at the moment of rebirth, when the Holy Spirit is "yielded and still," the Holy Spirit moves in to make His home and provide assistance for our pilgrimage with God. As we often read, Paul was an astute scholar of the works of the Old Testament. He was well aware of the fact that King David knew about the transforming quality of the indwelling Spirit. In Psalms 143:8, King David pleads with the Lord to "show me the way"— that is, be my guide, do not desert me, let your everlasting love remain with me.

Then in verse 9: "Rescue me from my enemies." He knows that it is the Spirit of God that enables and empowers us. Again, in verse 10: "Teach me to do your will, may your heart lead me to level ground." It is the Holy Spirit that explains our situations and places us in a position of divine understanding. Finally, in verse 11: "For your name's sake, O Lord, preserve my life, bring me out of trouble."

Yes, dear friend, it is God's Holy Spirit, whispering words of encouragement, and calling to our minds His mighty works that are done on our behalf. He removes discouragement and puts a song in our hearts. O yes, it is true—we must here and now bow our heads and our hearts and pray to the Holy Spirit to guide us, enable us, teach us, and comfort us. We must accept His assistance as we continue our earthly pilgrimage.

I ask you, shall we not meet the blessed Holy Spirit with the love He brings us and give in return our own deep and heartfelt love to Him? Let us turn to Him with our grateful love and plead: "Come Holy Spirit, Heavenly Dove, with all of Thy quickening powers. Kindle a flame of Scared Love, in these cold hearts of ours."

My dear Christian friend, let us take a moment here to dwell upon the message that the great Apostle Paul has for us in regard to our indwelling Holy Spirit. In Corinthians 6:19–20, we read, "What? Know you not that your body is the Temple of the Holy Spirit which is in you, which you have of God; and you are not your own? For you are bought with a price: Therefore, glorify God in your body and in your Spirit, which are God's!" Paul, in those few words, has made the message about as easy to understand as you will read anywhere. You and I have no right to live as we please. We should not live as we please. Why? Because the Lord Jesus has died for us, to redeem us from hell's misery. He has paid the price. Paul says, "God has bought you with the blood of His Son."

Paul is telling us two things in this message. There is a purchase price that has been paid, and there is a Holy Spirit within us. "Know you not that your body is the Temple of the Holy Spirit which is in you, which you have of God, and you are not your own." You see, God says we do not belong to ourselves, and the very moment we take faith in the blood of the Lord Jesus Christ, in that very moment, God sent forth the Spirit of His Son into our hearts.

Dear friend, God has sent the Holy Spirit into your heart to claim the territory that His Son purchased. Now, we all know that many of us refuse to listen to the pleading of the Holy Spirit. Why? Because we love ourselves to such a degree that we will not hand over the rights which the Holy Spirit claims for the Lord Jesus Christ. Well, it is a miserable life that we live—so miserable because we can never enjoy life until Jesus Christ possesses us.

This possession by Christ reminds me of the words *signed*, *sealed*, and *delivered*. This can be illustrated by a personal experience in my life.

One summer, I came home from college and was very fortunate to get a job working in a furniture factory (Crane and McMahon) in St. Marys, Ohio. My job was in the receiving department. Semi-truck loads of lumber came in daily from all over the United States. It was my specific duty to check each piece of lumber to make sure that our seal was burnt into it. The seal was vitally important because it absolutely proved that we had chosen, purchased, and paid for that particular piece of lumber.

My friend, God's seal is upon you! God has the right— His right—to govern, to rule through the entire length and breadth of your life. He pleads with you to surrender to Him as He reveals to you the glory of the Lord Jesus Christ. James 4:5 says, "That Spirit which He made to dwell in us, yearns for us, even unto jealous envy." He is pleading to gain the territory within our hearts that the Master has paid for with His life. He pleads for the rights of the Blessed Redeemer.

Truly, for the first twenty years of my life, I did pretty much as I pleased. But then, while I was a student at Heidelberg College, I met Rev. Charles Schwantes. His ministry was exactly what I needed. My life was transformed, and I surrendered my life to the Lord. I realized then that I had been robbing the Lord Jesus Christ, my Blessed Savior, of what was His, and my life was forever changed. I began then and there to live by the wisdom of God's Holy Word. I feel that world of difference that exists between being possessed and merely being the purchased property of someone.

For instance, a good friend of mine in Celina, Ohio had just bought a brand-new car. I was telling him how much I admired his new car, and he replied, "I wish I hadn't bought it!" "Why?" He said, "Ever since I bought that car, it is never here when I want it." "Where is it then?" I asked? "My wife loves it, and she always takes it."

Do you see the connection? He paid for it, but someone else is using it. You look upon the Cross of Calvary, and God will tell you by His Spirit that He paid for you and that He wants to possess you. And Paul is telling us, "You ought to be possessed by the One who purchased you!"

Let's you and I right now humbly acknowledge before God that He has paid the price and that He is forevermore the King of our life. Will you do that? We must deliberately decide, by the grace of God, to abandon the rule and reign of self. Let us take the crown from our own heads and place it where it belongs—on His!

If you will come to the place of absolute surrender, God can fill your soul with all of the blessed fullness of His Holy Spirit, and then you will go on your way rejoicing, knowing the Lord has met with you, and He will remain with you into eternity. As Paul said, "Present your bodies as a living sacrifice, holy, and acceptable to God." May the rest of your life be guided by the wisdom of the Living Word of God.

> By serving others with our gifts,
> And in telling everyone of his ways,
> By loving our fellow believers,
> And through our wonderful worshipful praise,
> By obeying and enjoying His Holy Word,
> Our focus is a marvelous reflection—
> Glorifying the life of Jesus Christ
> His death and His resurrection!
> Every martyr that ever was slain,
> Marched to the tune of the very same hymn,
> Delivering the message that we must maintain—
> It's not about us—it's about Him!
>
> —Russell Young

Prayer

O Lord, fill me with your Spirit today. Guide me, enable me, teach me, and comfort me. I need help as I continue my pilgrimage on the path to eternity. Amen.

The Good Shepherd

The Sheep were huddled beside the stream,
Quaking and trembling with fear.
A coyote was quietly approaching,
The scent telling them it was near.
With panic in their hearts, they clustered,
Squeezing in as close as they could,
For they realized they were defenseless,
With the predator in their neighborhood.

The shepherd soon heard their crying,
Was aware of the danger at hand,
By placing himself in the middle of the flock,
He restored peace to the frightened band.
With tenderness and solemn assurance
He quieted their timid souls,
And surrendering to his humble compassion,
They returned to the safety of the fold.

When you feel you've lost your direction,
Wondering when those heartaches will cease.
Turn, turn to your Savior, trust in Him
To render love, compassion, and peace.

Life can be frightful and challenging,
A safe haven will help you to perform,
The Good Shepherd can provide protection,
He is your anchor for every storm.

The Good Shepherd will draw near to defend you,
He'll be your shelter from evil and strife,
Surely His goodness and His mercies
Will surround you every day of your life!

—Russell Young

Epilogue

Dear friend, I pray that God has blessed you by the reading of this book. May the Holy Spirit that dwells within you find great joy and new strength in your journey to your heavenly abode. Let us pray that God will renew His blessings upon America and that she might return to the moral status that she enjoyed since her very beginning as a nation. I feel that we are living in an age of moral darkness and that we are approaching a slippery slope to degradation. We are in a desperate need for evangelists, for men of true Christian faith who will help to retrieve lost souls and bring our nation back to the wisdom and the power of the Holy Spirit that we enjoyed in the past centuries. Yes, my friend, we do need a revival of the Christian church. We must unite in this God-fearing, ever-loving Christian struggle.

God created all of us with a purpose. We have been richly blessed, deeply loved, and forgiven of all of our sins. Will you join us in the work of bringing this great nation to Jesus Christ? Help us to re-establish the way to Christian living—complete surrender to the Lord Jesus. Let your light shine! Help others to find Him and to draw ever nearer to Him. You were created for this purpose. He needs you now.

God bless you, and God bless America. Lead others to live in the wisdom of God's Holy Word. Amen.

About the Author

Russell Young is the author of two other books, *Living in His Kingdom, Stunned by His Grace* and *Glory Bound: Grace for the Journey*. He is a graduate of Memorial High School in St. Marys, Ohio. He has a bachelor's degree in Business Administration from Heidelberg University in Tiffin, Ohio and a dual master's degree in Retail Marketing/Guidance Counseling from St. Francis University in Fort Wayne, Indiana and Bowling Green State University in Bowling Green, Ohio. He was a missionary for three years in Ghana, West Africa, being a manager of two Presbyterian Church hospitals. He is a past president of the Auglaize County Retired Teachers. He and his wife, JoAnn, live in Van Wert, Ohio with their two children, Charles and Kathleen. Mr. Young has visited mission stations around the world, forty two countries in five continents, and recently toured China.